Held Fast for England

Kenyatta and the Politics of Kenya
The Last Bunker
Modern Nigeria
Britain's Oil

Photo: Peter Newbolt

G. A. HENTY

Held Fast for England

G. A. HENTY
IMPERIALIST BOYS' WRITER

BY

GUY ARNOLD

HAMISH HAMILTON
LONDON

First published in Great Britain 1980
by Hamish Hamilton Ltd
Garden House 57–59 Long Acre London WC2E 9JZ

Published in the United States of America by
Hamish Hamilton in association with
David and Charles Inc, North Pomfret, Vermont 05053, USA

British Library Cataloguing in Publication Data

Arnold, Guy
  Held fast for England.
  1. Henty, George Alfred – Criticism and
  interpretation
  I. Title
  823'.8   PR4785.H55
  ISBN 0-241-10373-8

Printed in Great Britain
by Ebenezer Baylis & Son Limited
The Trinity Press, Worcester, and London

To my father

Contents

Acknowledgements

I wish to acknowledge the help I have received in writing this book from members of the Henty Society (formed in 1977) whose interest and assistance with my researches have been invaluable. I am especially indebted to Roy Henty of 60 Painswick Road, Cheltenham (the Hon. Secretary of the Society), for his help in many ways; to Peter Newbolt for putting his knowledge at my disposal; to the Rev. Basil Brown for allowing me to use his magnificent library of Hentyana; and to all three for their hospitality.

GUY ARNOLD

The frontispiece is reproduced by courtesy of the Rev. Basil Brown and Peter Newbolt.

Preface

This is not a biography of Henty but an attempt to assess his importance and influence as a boys' writer. The first two chapters which are biographical are designed to put Henty into the perspective of the time in which he wrote. I have not attempted any in-depth biographical investigations of Henty and understand that a full-length biography is being prepared by William Allan, Editor of *The Connoisseur*.

Henty books (first editions) are now valuable collector's items and the Henty Society, formed in 1977, appears to attract a mixture of members: those who are primarily collectors of Hentyana; and those who still read him for amusement or to study the phenomenon of his success. Thirty years ago his principal publishers, Blackie, suggested his books for boys had then sold some 25 million copies and there have been further editions since that time.

Henty dominated the field of boys' writing from about 1880 to the First World War. It is, perhaps, not too difficult to see why he managed to lead the field for so long. Much the most interesting question in connexion with him is the extent to which the attitudes —about Britain, Empire, race—which come across so clearly in his writing influenced the generations of boys who read him, and it was my interest in his impact as an Imperial apologist which led me to write this book.

GUY ARNOLD
London, June 1979

PART ONE

Henty the Man

CHAPTER ONE

Henty's Life

GEORGE ALFRED HENTY was born at Trumpington, near Cambridge, on 8 December 1832; he died seventy years later on board his yacht *Egret* in Weymouth harbour on 16 November 1902. His life, therefore, spanned the Victorian era whose apogee at the time of Queen Victoria's two jubilees of 1887 and 1897 revealed the British at their most confident, their most powerful and most influential. In his attitudes and his writing Henty reflected the certainties of the Victorian age; he believed passionately in Britain's destiny and in his writing for boys constantly put forward what he considered to be the virtues which had made and would keep Britain great.

Today Henty is remembered as a boys' writer, yet he crammed into his life a great number of activities: he was soldier, miner, war correspondent, immensely travelled, yachtsman, popular clubman and literary figure who held strong views on many topics. George Manville Fenn, a contemporary boys' writer as well as friend of Henty, wrote a biography of Henty which was published in 1907. It is a curiously flat work which tells a great deal about Henty's activities and little about the man. Manville Fenn was writing a book about a recently passed heroic figure for boys and the picture he draws is not unlike that of one of Henty's own boy heroes in his many novels—though one that takes the story right through to death. There is a great deal about Henty's adventures, the out-of-way places he visited and the wars he covered but little to show what made Henty 'tick'.

Fenn called his book *The Story of an Active Life* which was apt enough; he also said in his preface that Henty believed in 'keeping himself to himself' and little is known about his private life, something that comes across again in the long essay on Henty by William Allan which appeared in the *Cornhill* magazine (No. 1082 1974/75).

There are mysteries about Henty's life in the sense that he very clearly divided it into two compartments: his public life which is well enough known and documented; and his private life which on the whole he appears to have kept to himself with remarkable success.

As a child Henty spent a great deal of his time ill in bed. In an interview for *The Captain* published in 1899 he said:

> I was a very weakly youngster, they did not expect me ever to see 'man's estate' at all. Until I was fourteen I was practically a confirmed invalid.

Henty's father, James, a stockbroker and mine-owner, appears to have been something of a roving man and a good deal of his restlessness communicated itself to his son. When Henty was five they moved to Canterbury and it was there over the next few years that he acquired his interest in plants and insects, an interest that is often apparent in the pages of his books. When over this period Henty was laid up in bed he read voraciously. At ten he went to school in London: a private school by Brompton Church run by a Mr. Pollard. At fourteen Henty went to Westminster School, and the school made a lasting impression upon Henty for it features in a number of his books. When he arrived at Westminster Henty was weak and sickly, he was interested in flowers and insects and foolishly let it be known that he wrote poetry; inevitably he was ragged and this led him to learn boxing in order to defend himself. In addition Westminster boys had to choose one of two sports—rowing or cricket—and Henty chose the former. The sickly child was to grow into a powerful man whose skill at boxing he would put to the test in many parts of the world. It must have been at Westminster that a number of influences coalesced in Henty to produce the ideal that he subsequently put forward so consistently in his boys' stories. On the one hand he was already extremely well read for a boy of his age and this combined with his botanical and poetry interests produced the gentler, writing side of his nature; on the other hand the rough and tumble pressures of the school ensured the manly, boxing, tough side which was to stand him in such good stead during his twenty years of travel as a correspondent. Henty, whose humour has been described as of the practical kind, could sometimes be more subtle and in the opening of his story, *By Sheer Pluck*, he combines in the hero, Hargate, the two aspects of his own nature that must have warred with each other during his Westminster days. The book begins almost whimsically:

'Now, Hargate, what a fellow you are! I've been looking for you everywhere. Don't you know it's the House against the Town boys. It's lucky that the town have got the first innings; they began a quarter of an hour ago.'

'How tiresome!' Frank Hargate said: 'I was watching a most interesting thing here. Don't you see this little chaffinch nest in the bush, with a newly hatched brood. There was a small black snake. . . .'

Reluctantly the hero leaves watching nature and returns to take part in the school cricket match; after the Captain of the school he is the most popular boy who played 'a steady rather than a brilliant game', a phrase that could well be applied to Henty himself. Hargate saves the match so his dilettante pursuit is overlooked.

This passage tells us a good deal about Henty and though in his later books his heroes have become all too machine-like there are often some delicate touches in his earlier stories. In *The Young Franc-Tireurs*, for example, Henty describes a scene of touching pathos. In the middle of a battle Percy, one of the two brother heroes of the book, is galloping across a field after delivering a message:

Suddenly he came upon a sight which, hurried as he was, and exposed as was the position, caused him instantly to draw his rein, and come to a full stop. There in the open field were two children. The one a boy of six or seven years old, the other a little flaxen-haired blue-eyed girl of five. They were quietly picking flowers.

Westminster made a substantial impact upon Henty. There is an account of life at the school in his early adult novel, *All But Lost*; his story about the French Revolution, *In the Reign of Terror*, is sub-titled 'The Adventures of a Westminster Boy'; while the hero of *Captain Bayley's Heir* is at Westminster when the story opens and the school features quite prominently in that book.

Henty went to Caius College, Cambridge, in 1852 where for a year he read Classics and rowed for his college eight. He also took boxing lessons from a retired professional middleweight, Nat Langham, and before he was twenty he had learnt to wrestle, his

teacher being Jamieson of Newcastle, a one-time champion of the
Cumberland style. Both his boxing and wrestling he later put to
good use when among the camp-followers of Garibaldi in Italy or
in a Californian mining camp. He collapsed at the end of his first
year after three weeks of intensive study and so went down for a
year. During that time he stayed in Wales where his father had a
coal mine and iron works. Here, clearly, Henty gained the knowledge which he was to put to practical use later: in Sardinia and
California where he again became involved in mining; in Italy
during the Austro-Italian War of 1866 when he claimed to be an
engineer and so got himself aboard the Italian fleet in Ancona after
the battle of Lissa to study the effects of gunfire on ironclads; and
in his book *Facing Death*.

He returned to Cambridge but shortly afterwards, when the
Crimean War began, Henty was offered an appointment in the
Commissariat Department of the army which he took up, leaving
university for good and embarking upon the twenty or so years of
his military and war correspondent days. Although he read Classics
at Cambridge Henty claimed that he learnt good, every-day
colloquial Latin at Westminster. In a number of his books he makes
his boys bad at Latin and Greek and, indeed, often says it is unimportant or unnecessary for them since they are off to be soldiers
or adventurers of one kind or another. Yet in his interview in *The
Captain* in 1899 Henty says of his Latin:

> When I went out to the Crimea, and, later, to Italy, I found
> that every-day Latin perfectly invaluable. It was the key to
> modern Italian—and a very good key, too. But more than that,
> it meant that wherever I could come across a priest I had a
> friend and an interpreter.

Although Henty often plays down Latin in his books he invariably
makes his heroes learn a language and often has them praised for
doing so by some more senior character in the story.

His Crimean experiences made a great impact upon Henty: in
the Purveyor's Department of the Army he discovered every sort
of incompetence—he was concerned with provisions, the supply
of medicines and the administration of army hospitals. One may
wonder whether any of the conditions he brought to light helped
persuade Florence Nightingale to go to the Crimea. He was highly
critical of what he saw and wrote such criticisms home, leading

his father to approach the editor of the *Morning Advertiser* and suggest that his son should contribute regular accounts of conditions in the army. This, then, was the beginning of Henty's career as a war correspondent.

The general state of disorganization throughout the British army at the time of the Crimean War soon became notorious and the fact that this was when Henty, as an impressionable young man, became familiar with military affairs undoubtedly affected his later approach as a writer: he might be an exponent of British greatness and military heroism; he could also be unsparing of incompetence. Organizing the wretched Purveyor's Department gave Henty a taste for order—he was promoted purveyor of the forces after being invalided home from the war—so that a feature of his young heroes in most of his novels is their readiness and ability to organize their fellows.

Henty's brother, Frederick, joined him in the Crimea but tragically died of cholera within a fortnight of his arrival, an event that deeply affected Henty and helped make him ill, leading to his return to England. *Jack Archer*, an early Henty novel, is about the Crimean War: it is one of his better stories, containing some gentle and perceptive comments on war. It has two brothers as heroes and this brother pattern recurs in a number of Henty's stories.

Henty was to remain in the army for a total of five years and was stationed first in Belfast, where he took up the sport of yachting, and later in Portsmouth when he was in charge of the whole South-West of England. In 1859 he went to Italy to organize the hospitals of the Italian Legion during the war with Austria.

Henty had married Elizabeth Finucane while he was still in the army and their first child, Charles Gerald, was born in October 1858. There was a second son, Hubert, and two daughters, but Elizabeth died in 1865 aged only twenty-nine. It was a major blow to Henty who then turned to journalism as a full-time occupation. Meanwhile, he had had a further abortive attempt at mining, this time silver, in Sardinia, and had got to know Garibaldi. Little, however, is known of his activities during the first half of the 1860s.

Henty's career as a war correspondent really began with the Austro-Italian War of 1866 which he covered for the *Standard*; he met the novelist George Meredith who was covering the war for the *Morning Post* and on one occasion when too near the lines was mistaken for a spy. Henty had a high regard for the fighting potential of Garibaldi's soldiers; he found more than once that he needed his boxing skill and on one occasion staged a contest with Meredith for the benefit of Garibaldi and his followers.

For the next ten years Henty was to appear in half the war zones of the world as he went to cover a wide variety of campaigns for the *Standard*. Manville Fenn claims that his private letters were uninteresting and that only his published material had any value. This may well be true, and revelations about the private lives of public men often, in fact, reveal nothing, yet Fenn does manage to convey the impression that there was more to Henty's private life than the bare published details would indicate, though that was not his intention. Apart from saying that yachting had become Henty's principal hobby Fenn tells almost nothing of his private life.

After Italy the next major expedition upon which Henty embarked was Lord Napier's to Abyssinia in 1867–68; subsequently his despatches were published as *The March to Magdala* in 1868. He had already published his first adult novel, *A Search for a Secret*, in 1867. The next year he wrote his first boys' book, *Out on the Pampas*, although it was not published until 1871. He devised the story to tell to his own children and the four children in the Hardy family, Charles, Hubert, Maud and Ethel, have the same names as Henty's.

Henty appears to have enjoyed the Magdala expedition: he lived well, he wrote excellent despatches and obtained much good copy. The next major event he covered was the Franco-Prussian War of 1870–71 (although in 1869 he had attended the opening of the Suez Canal and then travelled in both Egypt and Palestine). He first went to Berlin and saw the war from the Prussian side, his despatches among other things drawing a distinction between the military might of Europe and the military unpreparedness of Britain. Although he started favourably disposed towards the Germans he lost this enthusiasm as the war went on and was to write:

> For more than a quarter of a century Europe was convulsed by the ambition of France: is it to be that we are doomed to a quarter of a century's war or preparations for war because of the ambition of Germany?

He returned briefly to England, obtained fresh accreditation and funds and then went back to the war, but this time to see it from the French side. Of all his boys' books, *The Young Franc-Tireurs* is the only one that draws consistently and sometimes precisely upon the materials which Henty accumulated as a war correspondent.

Henty was in Paris during the period of the Commune and what he witnessed then deeply impressed him; it was at this time that he developed a scorn for the mob which periodically surfaces in his books. He described the Communards as a savage rabble, he attacked their hypocrisy, cowardice and bravado. He was, however, equally scornful of the vicious reprisals taken by the middle classes against the Commune once it had collapsed:

> But what I do say is, that thousands have been sacrificed without their executioners taking the trouble to ascertain their identity. The clamour of the mob was considered to be sufficient proof of guilt.

The Crimean and Franco-Prussian Wars were the two military events in which Henty took part that made the deepest and most lasting impressions upon him.

Henty was next in Russia for the campaign in the Turkoman War which included the siege of Khiva. Henty never got to the siege but he did collect a great amount of material, some of which provided the background for his two Russian-based books (apart from *Jack Archer*), *Through Russian Snows* and *Condemned as a Nihilist*. Almost as soon as he had returned from this trip, Henty was off again to follow Sir Garnet Wolseley to the Gold Coast for the Ashanti campaign of 1873–74. The campaign again provided Henty with a considerable quantity of background detail: apart from his despatches he wrote *The March to Coomassie* (1874) and ten years later produced his boys' book, *By Sheer Pluck*.

Henty met H. M. Stanley during this campaign and they went on a hazardous sailing excursion down the coast. Wolseley disliked war correspondents as a breed yet he and Henty became friends and subsequently dining companions, though Henty did not always agree with Wolseley when he was introducing his army reforms.

Between 1874 (the end of the Ashanti War) and 1876 Henty went on three more major expeditions: first to Spain to cover the Carlist insurrection of 1874 (his experiences gave him material for one of his later boys' books, *With the British Legion*, published in 1903); he

was then to accompany the Prince of Wales on his visit to India in
1875, a lengthy tour that no doubt provided much of the background
and colour for his series of books about India; and thirdly he was
off again to Serbia for the Turco-Serbian War of 1876. His health,
however, now broke down, and except for a visit to California in
1885 when he examined mining camps his travelling days were over.

The remainder of Henty's life was devoted to writing books,
and though he produced a dozen adult novels his real métier was
writing the boys' stories upon which much of his reputation rests.
He did a good deal of public speaking and often chaired meetings;
he was a 'club' man and for many years the most popular, or
notable, member of the Savage. His hobby was yachting and he
purchased a sixteen-tonner, graduated to a thirty-two-tonner and
finished up with the *Egret* which was of eighty-three tons. In 1889
he married his housekeeper, Elizabeth Keylock, who survived him;
the marriage was the cause of controversy and bitterness.

Henty was a gourmet and enjoyed the good things of life. When
on the Abyssinian expedition under Napier, for example, he had his
own Indian servants and did himself well. He describes a meal
they prepared for him on the march as consisting of soup, sheep's
face grilled with tongue and brain sauce, mutton, jugged hare,
omelettes and honey. Napier remarked that if one wanted a good
meal Henty was the man to go to.

He had a reputation as an exceptionally hard worker who paid
great attention to detail and was always ready to help other writers
and beginners, and remarked that, when he was approached by
would-be writers who clearly could not write, 'I let them down
as lightly as I can.' Asked about a love interest in his boys' stories
Henty said:

> No, I never touch a love interest. Once I ventured to make a boy
> of twelve kiss a little girl of eleven, and I received a very indignant
> letter from a dissenting minister.

The claim in fact is not true; in most of his boys' stories he marries
the hero off at the conclusion and in some, at least, there are quite
interesting love passages (within the conventions of Henty's time)
and it is possible to play the game of 'spot the girl'—usually fourteen
years of age when she first appears—whom the hero will ultimately
marry.

By the latter part of his life Henty had become something of an institution. He was a big, burly, bluff, bearded man described as of athletic figure and weighing seventeen stone, although he had spent years of his childhood and youth delicate and ill and claimed that at Cambridge he was a walking skeleton. He was of irascible temper and there are many stories of his rows with colleagues and publishers. Henty's association with Wolseley was important for he was to write for the *Standard* on military topics. He edited or helped edit three boys' magazines. In 1880 he took over the editorship of *Union-Jack* from W. H. G. Kingston; from 1888 to 1890 he edited Beeton's *Boys' Own Magazine* and, starting in 1889 with Archibald Forbes, produced a boys' annual, *Camps and Quarters*. None did well.

Henty's second marriage was clearly a social disaster. He was then living in Battersea and engaged Elizabeth Keylock as his housekeeper. His two unmarried sons were also living with him. There were, apparently, constant domestic rows and the two sons objected to her; but then Henty married her after being a widower for twenty-four years. She was the daughter of a farmer, coarse, socially below Henty and strong-willed. Three years after the marriage Henty's sister, Mary Bovill, died and this loss hurt the Hentys for she had brought up his children after the death of their mother and was deeply loved by them. Henty appears to have quarrelled with both his sons though the breach with the elder, Charles, was healed. The younger, Hubert, went out to California where he died in 1908. A number of suggestions have been made as to a social scandal that led Hubert to emigrate though no one has recorded just what it amounted to. Manville Fenn did not even mention the second marriage in his biography. Clearly the reactions of both family and friends to his second wife did much to embitter Henty in his last years so that his irascibility was accentuated and a hardness crept into some of his writing, which is quite noticeable in the ruthlessness with which he invests some of his boy heroes in his final dozen novels. W. O. G. Lofts has looked in some depth at what he calls 'The Biographical Mysteries of George Alfred Henty'.*

Many journalists of his day paid tribute to Henty as a writer, a war correspondent and as a 'clubabble man': he was for years chairman of the Savage Club and belonged to the Whitefriars Club and the Royal Thames Yacht Club and was a Chief Brave of the

* *Dime Novel Round-Up*, April 1977.

Wigwam, a small dining club which held cultural evenings and had been formed by members of the Savage Club who had become bored with the latter's cuisine. Although he worked hard Henty also played equally hard. In his latter years he claimed that he spent only six months writing his three boys' books and the other six on his yacht. He took part a number of times in the race from Dover to Heligoland for the Kaiser's Cup, although he never succeeded in winning it.

Like many journalists Henty almost certainly wrote a good deal of anonymous material and it is at least possible that he edited other papers than the three mentioned above. Again, according to Lofts, it is possible that Henty contributed anonymously to *The Boy's Friend*. More important, despite his huge output, he was often short of money and worried by its absence.

Henty had a Tory image although there are some surprisingly liberal sentiments in a number of his books and in one of his last, *With the Allies to Pekin*, for example, he inveighs against what he calls 'the policy of grab' in China. Outspoken, forceful and choleric, he had as many enemies as friends (possibly one of the nicest antipathetic comments upon him, quoted in William Allan's 'G. A. Henty' from the *Cornhill* Magazine, came from Dr. Gordon Stables who also published with Blackie and on one of his visits 'noted with repugnance the presence of that "stiff, dogmatic old pagan George Henty" '). For the last eight years of his life he lived at 33 Lavender Gardens, Battersea. His health declined in his last year and he cruised in southern waters for the summer preceding his death. He died aboard his yacht, the *Egret*, on 16 November 1902.

In one of the many obituaries appeared this much-quoted letter from an American boy:

> Dear Mr. Henty,—I am an American boy. My father brought me to London and showed me the Tower and St. Paul's. Then I asked him to show me Mr. Henty. He took me to Mr. Blackie's office, and the gentleman there told us you lived in Putney. Dear Mr. Henty, I should so much like to see you.

Henty left his house and contents to his wife, except for 'The Library' which went to his son Charles, while royalties were to be paid to his wife and sons at a fixed rate. The gross value of his published will was £6,035 19s. 7d.

One of the earliest mentions of Henty in a journalistic capacity must be that in a letter from William Howard Russell, the famous Crimean correspondent, to Delane, editor of *The Times*: 'The new correspondent of the *Morning Post* is a purveyor's clerk named Henty.' George Steiner, in his book *Tolstoy or Dostoevsky*, also mentions Henty in connexion with the Crimea but in a more flattering light:

. . . and to G. A. Henty, who, like Tolstoy, was profoundly marked by his experiences in the Crimea.

A good many writers mention Henty as a friend, colleague or acquaintance, for his years as a war correspondent brought him into contact with an enormous range of men. The mentions are often brief as that by George Augustus Sala in his autobiography when he says he came across Henty in Italy covering the Garibaldi campaign. Or they are warmer and more interesting. In his book *Sixty Years in the Wilderness* Henry W. Lucy tells how he got to know Henty during the miners' coal strike of 1873 in Wales which Henty covered for the *Standard*. Lucy says of him: 'He was at once the warmest-hearted, shortest-tempered man in the world.' He tells how they played cards with the telegraph clerk sent from London to deal with all their messages (the clerk drank port with his pork, and then trumped Henty's king when the ace had gone so that 'Henty jumped to his feet and threw his cards on the table exclaiming "My God" ').

At that time Henty was trying to supplement his income as a journalist by the recovery of tin from broken or disused utensils— without much success. Henty built a reversible boat that was bound to right itself, but it kept turning over and leaving Henty in the river. Years later, Lucy says, he met Henty who invited him for a weekend on his yawl, but Henty had by then developed 'a somewhat embarrassing habit of prodding you, so to speak, with his corpora- tion' and the thought of Henty in a small boat following him round to make a point was too much for Lucy. It is a sad little picture.

Another correspondent, M. Prior, says (in his *Campaigns of a War Correspondent*) that Henty befriended him when he went to follow Wolseley's Ashanti-Coomassie campaign and was very help- ful. They watched a lizard kill a mouse and Henty promptly wrote a piece about sucking blood. In another book, *A Sheaf of Memoirs* by Frank Scudamore, Henty's name crops up in connexion with correspondents in the Balkans. In these and many other references Henty comes across as a forceful, often dominant personality; in Henty's stories the heroes are habitually didactic and tend to lay down the law to their associates, quite apart from what they may do to their enemies.

Henty was often approached by young hopefuls who wanted his advice or encouragement to become writers. The way Henty dealt with such requests is described by George Bainton in *The Art of Authorship*. Henty maintained that no teaching would make a writer and said: 'The number of boys with an instinct for writing is small.' He advises beginners to try a story and then get someone they trust to look at it: 'If he says no, give the thing up altogether. If he says yes . . . then write, and write, and write. Burn all you write, for until you are two or three and twenty you will certainly not write anything worth reading.'

The *Union-Jack*, which Henty edited, did not last long despite the eminence as boys' writers of both Henty and his predecessor, W. H. G. Kingston. As Kingston's biographer said dryly: 'One gets the impression that, unless there is either substantial backing or a powerful printing house behind the undertaking, continuity is hardly possible.' When Kingston turned over the editorship of the *Union-Jack* to Henty, the latter wrote in the magazine:

> I am an example of a boy who has got his wish; for I have often thought that I would, above all things, in the way of literary work, like to edit a magazine for boys. The editor of a boys' magazine should have a great liking for and a keen sympathy with boys. He should have the art of putting himself in their place, and of feeling what they feel, and liking what they like. In this way only can he choose the stories that will take. For a story may be excellent in itself, admirable in tone, well written and with plenty of plot, and yet it may fail altogether with boys, simply because, as they would say themselves, it does not suit them.
>
> I suffer at a disadvantage in succeeding so old and tried a friend of boys as your late editor—his name was of itself a tower of strength—but he has promised to continue to write for you, and will aid me with his advice.

But Kingston died shortly afterwards.

One of Henty's books published in 1897 was *With Cochrane the*

Dauntless; Henty considered Cochrane a genius who had been misunderstood and badly treated by his country:

> Then followed one of the most disgraceful parodies of justice ever performed in this country. Lord Cochrane was arrested, tried, and by means of a partisan judge, false evidence, and measures more unscrupulous even than those of Judge Jeffreys, convicted and sentenced to imprisonment.

When Henty was partisan few holds were barred. The judge in question was Lord Ellenborough and his grandson, J. B. Atlay, then produced a 500-page book *Lord Cochrane's Trial before Lord Ellenborough*, to refute attacks upon his grandfather (not merely Henty's). He says, for example: '. . . and a novelist of the stamp of Mr. G. A. Henty, apparently believes in the truthfulness of the statements . . .' Later in the book he asks whether justice in 1814 had sunk to the level of the Bloody Assizes:

> For this is really what Lord Campbell and the autobiographers of a Seaman, and Mr. Henty, and those who recklessly followed their statements, charged Lord Ellenborough with. They may soften it down and call it 'political rancour'—though to do Mr. Henty justice he goes in boldly for the comparison to Jeffreys . . .

Henty more than once was at the centre of some such storm.

A few other references to Henty that appeared in other men's memoirs are worth mentioning. Douglas Sladen in *Twenty Years of My Life* (published in 1914) describes Henty as a good club chairman, a bluff personality who had been a power among correspondents and adds:

> Henty's work as a war correspondent gave him the copy for those wonderful books which made him the boys' Dumas. He was a great personality, and, as I saw, on the only two occasions when I ran across him in a crisis, a born leader of men.

Unfortunately he does not tell us what the two crises were.

Edward McCourt in a biography—*Remember Butler*—published in 1967 says:

> Henty wrote from two to six juveniles a year for more than a quarter of a century; and if one accepts the premise on which most of his stories are founded, that England can do no wrong, what

follows is a most entertaining mixture of exciting adventure and surprisingly accurate history.

Henty crops up in the autobiographical sketches of Sir John Furley, *In Peace and War*, for they had been friends and were together in Paris during the Commune in 1870–71. In *An Editor Looks Back*, by George A. L. Green, published in 1947, the author reminisces:

> Among the visiting press celebrities of those days, most of whose names I have forgotten, was George Henty, the famous writer of books for boys who, in his blue double-breasted suit looked like an engineer in the mercantile marine. Proudly I strutted by his side when my father took him for a walk on Southsea Clarence Esplanade pier.

Shortly after Henty's death Robert Overton dedicated his book *Dangerous Days* 'To the Memory of G. A. Henty The Friend and Mentor of British Boys all the world over.' He received the following letter from Mrs. Henty which he published with the dedication:

> My dear Mr. Robert Overton,—
> With the keenest appreciation I welcome your intention of dedicating 'Dangerous Days' to the memory of my dear late husband. He kept to the last that same great tender heart so easily moved by the sorrows of others, and by kindly deeds. Your proposal, in friendship's name, to dedicate your next book to him gave him great pleasure during his last days; and now in my grief I, too, thank you much for so valued a tribute to his memory.

Finally, perhaps, one can refer to *A Critical History of Children's Literature* published by Macmillan in 1969. In it there is a sympathetic and fair appraisal of Henty and then a quotation from Samuel Crother's *Miss Muffet's Christmas Party* about Henty boys: 'There seem to be a great many of them, but I've sometimes thought there may be only two, only they live in different centuries and go to different wars.'

CHAPTER TWO

Impact and Reputation

AT THE BEGINNING of his bibliography of Henty, Robert Dartt*
gives a quotation by W. G. Blackie about the sales of Henty's books:

> I would say that he was the most popular Boys' author of his
> day. Certainly I was brought up to believe that Henty was Boys'
> Author No. 1 of his time . . . The figure of 150,000 [copies] a
> year in the days of his popularity I do not think can be under
> the mark . . . I know that with our figure [some 3,514,000 printed
> and presumably sold], Scribner's, and Donohue's plus an un-
> known quantity for other pirated editions, it looks as if 25,000,000
> is not impossible.

Henty's earlier books were published by Griffith and Farran,
Sampson Low, and Routledge, and books by these publishers
appeared between 1871 and 1885. Blackie first published a Henty
in 1882 (*Facing Death*) but there was to be an overlap with other
publishers for a few years, until Henty had discharged his obliga-
tions, and before Blackie had tied Henty down to write only for
them. A letter from Blackie to Henty dated 14 May 1887, sets out
to clarify discussions that had taken place between the two. The
first point made is:

> That for the period of five years from this date, that is to say
> until April 1892 Mr George A. Henty undertakes to write books
> designed for young people for Messrs. Blackie and Son only and
> in consideration of this Messrs. Blackie and Son agree to accept
> from Mr Henty each year three (3) Books written for young
> people:— Each Book to contain from 90 to 120,000 words, and
> Messrs. Blackie shall pay Mr. Henty for each of these books the
> sum of £100 (Hundred pounds sterling).

* *G. A. Henty, A Bibliography*, John Sherratt & Son, 1971.

In a new contract of 1891—after four rather than five years—
the length of book has increased to between 100,000 and 140,000
words and the advance on each to £150. This contract is interesting
for the details it also contains of royalties payable for other Henty
titles already on Blackie's lists: 3½d. a copy on those appearing in the
6s. series (eight are listed), 3d. a copy on those in the 5s. series (nine
are listed), again 3½d. a copy on another ten titles at 6s. but only
when they had sold an initial 5,000 copies, and 3d. a copy on four
more titles when these had passed the 5,000 mark.

Henty books were immensely popular in the United States, but
until 1891 and the International Copyright Act pirating in America
was on a huge scale:

In America, in the decades following the end of the Civil War
in 1865, cheap paper was abundant, international copyright was
non-existent, and, among lesser publishers and booksellers,
savage price-cutting and competition became at first an essential
to survival in business and later an easy form of commercial
suicide. Small publishers vied with each other for, and, paradoxi-
cally, sometimes shared amongst each other, material suitable to
feed into the cheap stores. Successful British authors, with no
legal protection in the States, were profitable, sitting targets.

In the circumstances it was inevitable that Henty's books
would be produced in large quantities in America. Between about
1885 and 1920 approximately fifty American houses published
pirated editions of them; some specific titles could be obtained
from at least sixteen publishers. The piracy of course included
books from Henty's other publishers, not just Blackie, and a
number of them appeared with new and unfamiliar titles. There
is no doubt that Henty's readers in America, often, though not
always, of volumes vilely printed and bound to disintegrate, must
have been legion. Nor can there be much doubt that, while Henty
and his British publishers made nothing out of these sales the
pirates were working in such cheap and nasty competition with
each other that their own profit margins were very small indeed.
In March 1889, Blackie agreed to pay Henty royalties on sheets
sold to America: this was an innovation as they were still only
making him down payments for the British rights. It is probable,
however, that in the face of cut-throat competition the sales of
any such authorised American editions were minimal.

In 1891 the International Copyright Act was passed. In September of the same year Blackie made a new agreement with Henty, increasing the down payments by fifty per cent and also giving him a royalty on British sales over 5,000 copies of each book. The royalty on sheets exported to America was confirmed, and Henty was to share equally with Blackie such royalties as might be obtained from newly authorized Scribner editions now for the first time to be printed in the States.*

Thus in 1892 Charles Scribner's Sons paid royalties on the sales of cheap editions of Henty's books on the following scale: of three books, an annual average sale of *With Clive in India* (1,991), *In the Reign of Terror* (1,994) and *One of the 28th* (1,987), making for that year a total of 5,972. The same company, in the six years 1895 to 1900, sold the following averages and totals of ten Henty titles (*With Clive in India, In the Reign of Terror, One of the 28th, Under Drake's Flag, In Freedom's Cause, The Lion of St. Mark, With Wolfe in Canada, With Lee in Virginia, By Pike and Dyke* and *By England's Aid*): 1895, an average of 329 copies of each title (total 3,293); 1896, an average of 2,335 (total 23,357); 1897, an average of 3,180 (total 31,806); 1898, an average of 2,564 (total 25,644); 1899, an average of 635 (total 6,352); and 1900, an average of 1,089 (total 10,896)—making 101,148 all together. There were other priced editions in the market at the same time.

It would seem, moreover, that Henty's popularity as a medium for teaching history in American junior schools lasted in some instances very nearly down to the present time, whereas his appeal waned considerably earlier in Britain. Eric Quayle claims in *The Collector's Book of Boys' Stories*:

The debt the late-Victorian and Edwardian educationalists owed to G. A. Henty as a popular historian was often acknowledged in later years, when the boys who had devoured his historical tales had grown to manhood.

This seems also to have been the case in the United States as well as in Canada, Australia and New Zealand. In Britain, however, as late as 1955 Henty was being reproduced in the Collins Schoolboys' Library, No. 9 of the series being *One of the 28th*.

---

* The above passage was written specifically for me by Peter Newbolt to whom I am indebted for this and other information appearing in this book.

Henty books today have great attraction as collector's items and first editions are much sought after, the rarest fetching considerable prices: the Blackie editions with their olivine edges, blocked covers and illustrations make most attractive trophies as well as having a high and increasing value. The stories are also a rich source of material for anyone studying attitudes in Victorian England, no matter what the period of a particular story might be.

It was not until J. A. Blackie took Henty over in the 1880s that he began to make his mark and, more important perhaps, make some money. Blackie played a major part in the renaissance of children's literature and Henty was the first of a number of writers whose works, though containing 'sound moral precepts', concentrated upon adventure and in Henty's case history rather than sin and sermonizing. Boys' writers from the middle to the end of the last century such as Kingsley, Ballantyne, Kingston, Fenimore Cooper or Manville Fenn each had their own following though none would appear to have rivalled Henty in popularity. Some writers (not specifically boys' writers) may have produced one or more outstanding titles upon which much of their subsequent reputation rested— *Kidnapped* or *The Coral Island*; none however became quite the institution that Henty did during his lifetime to the extent that towards the end he was approached and interviewed about the mysteries of writing for boys as though he alone had the secret, while reviewers habitually referred to him as the leading exponent of the art.

Henty showed a suitable awareness of his special position in the final years before his death when, more than in his earlier days, he tended to preach. The last magazine article he wrote was called 'True Heroism: A Talk with the Boys' and appeared in the *Home Messenger*, Volume XII, January to December 1903. He starts by saying that there is hardly a boy (and few girls) who does not in his heart want to be a hero; and then says that everyone has it in his power to influence others. The two main qualities Henty picks out are, first, truthfulness and, second, unselfishness. When he has expatiated upon both qualities, and then added a paragraph upon how women can be true heroes, Henty finishes by saying that to be a true hero you must be a true Christian: 'True heroism is inseparable from true Christianity, and as a step towards the former I would urge, most strongly and urgently the practice of the latter.'

This was a reflective Henty piece; often, however, there is an abrasive quality about some of his contributions to magazines, a tendency which was perhaps a factor in ensuring that he had no particular success as an editor. In the July 1890 issue of *Boys' Own Magazine* he deals with the subject of strikes: ' "In the Workshops" has asked me if I would tell boys what I think of strikes. I am glad to do so.' He proceeds at considerable length to lecture his young readers as to the merits or otherwise of striking. It is, perhaps, interesting that in his opening paragraph he says that the question of strikes is one of the most important subjects affecting the interests of the country's workers. He continues:

> And it would be a very good thing if every lad could have some sound advice on the subject, so that when he takes his place among the army of workers he may be able to think for himself, instead of being swayed by men who are often blinded by passion, or capable of seeing only one side of the question.

Henty is here addressing his remarks to boys who might be workers and strikers themselves, whereas he once claimed that his books' historical content had influenced boys to join the army—but mainly as officers. In both *Through the Fray* and *Facing Death*,* although showing sympathy for certain aspects of the lives of the working people he portrays, Henty comes down very clearly against strikes, and in *Facing Death* makes the hero, himself a working-class boy, break a strike.

This particular article clearly caused offence for in the October issue of the magazine Henty is back on the same subject:

> I have had two or three letters from boys saying that their fathers object strongly to what I have said upon the subject of strikes. I am not at all surprised at that; it is a marked characteristic of the day that men have a strong tendency to look at matters from only one point of view, and to refuse to listen for a moment to the arguments of those who differ from them.

He goes on in this vein, indeed he becomes more abrasive, echoing with total obstinacy the tone of which he complains. However, he concludes his long editor's reply fairly enough:

> If in politics, in the discussion of social questions, and, above all, in what may be called working men's questions, men would but

* See Chapter twelve.

2

listen to arguments on both sides, and try to arrive at a fair and dispassionate conclusion as to what is fair and just, things would work far more pleasantly and far more happily in these islands of ours.

Henty certainly did not write down to his boys although his habitual 'My dear lads' with which he began all his prefaces might be deemed condescending; sometimes, however, he gives the impression of a tetchiness when dealing with the queries presumably of twelve- or thirteen-year-olds that was hardly the best manner for a boys' magazine editor to adopt. In one of his books Henty talks of the easy relations between boys and their fathers in Victorian times as opposed to the period of which he was writing; he would, one imagines, be horrified by such relations in the Britain of the 1970s.

It is the fate of people far more eminent than Henty to be denigrated in the years following their deaths and Henty certainly had his detractors. In the May 1908 issue of *The Captain* a strong attack was made upon him for the attitudes he had encouraged in his writing, and though the long letter, entitled 'Concerning Englishmen' from a Mr. R. van Eeghen (clearly a foreigner), is exaggerated, it makes a good many points that were to be more generally levelled against writers such as Henty only after a lapse of many more years when the climate in Britain had changed far more drastically. Van Eeghen begins:

There is no doubt that the immortal Henty and his hosts of imitators have made the British nation the most conceited people on this earth. It is the plotless trash of authors who shelter themselves behind the section in the library catalogue entitled 'Books for Boys', which has given the average young Englishman that very excellent opinion of himself which he now enjoys. Putting aside the question of the utter impossibilities of the usual boys' book, it is quite easy to see the harm the authors of these volumes cause by the exaggeration of the deeds and opinions of their *invraisemblables* heroes. After fourteen or fifteen years perusal of 'piffle' written apparently for his edification, the young Englishman leaves home and country with the very firm idea in his head that he, personally, is equal to two or more Frenchmen, about four Germans, an indefinite number of Russians, and any quantity you care to mention of the remaining scum of the earth.

There is a good deal more of the same, van Eeghen saying at one point: 'All this because of Messrs. Henty and Co.'s zeal to show him [the young Englishman] that the earth was made for England.' This refreshingly vituperative foreigner concludes:

> You may boast of the loyalty of the Colonies, but note the expression in an Englishman's voice when he tells you that So-and-So is a 'colonial' . . . Henty and Co. have done more to endanger the Empire than the blunders of many statesmen whom we could name.

Inevitably this drew an equally vituperative response, from a Mr. Bernard G. T. Hawkes, who to rub salt into van Eeghen's wounds says, among many other things:

> An Englishman was popularly supposed to be the *equal* of two Frenchman, I have never come across anything to justify the latter part of the statement, the nearest approach being that after Blake's victory over van Tromp, popular opinion magnified an Englishman into being equal to four *Dutchmen*.

More important, however, Hawkes defends Henty the writer:

> For although Mr. Henty did not, perhaps, possess the same power of creating character as other writers of fiction, yet his literary efforts are far from being the 'plotless trash' which our friend describes them to be. As Mr. Henty so often states in the preface of his books, his chief endeavours were directed, not so much towards writing fiction, as towards teaching boys history in a form interesting and acceptable to them; and I think many young men will be with me when I say that I learnt far more history by reading Mr. Henty's tales than I ever had crammed into me at school.

Hawkes makes the point that many others have raised: that Henty succeeded as a teacher of history. Van Eeghen is more interesting, despite his exaggerations, for raising the subtler issue: Henty may have taught history (though van Eeghen does not concede this) but what other attitudes did he also teach and how much damage did these do?

Henty the teacher of history is certainly a recurring theme as the following passage taken from an affectionate Fourth Leader in *The Times* in 1950 shows:

It is, indeed, one of the remarkable features of these works that the titles remain so clear and everything else is so dim. *In Times of Peril* was the Indian Mutiny and *By Sheer Pluck* Ashanti, *With Clive in India* and *The Young Carthaginian* explain themselves. *St. George for England* was surely Crecy, or was it by chance Agincourt? It is easy enough to reel off those lovely names, but what was it all about? Not so much as the ghost of an incident remains. Yet something does remain—namely, a little, a very little, history.

Henty contributed to many journals apart from the papers for which he wrote. A piece by him—'Baggage Under Difficulties'— appeared in Dickens' weekly, *All the Year Round*, of 15 August 1868, while the next issue of 22 August featured another Henty piece, not signed, called 'Sixty-Eight in Abyssinia', which is the story of the Abyssinian campaign told through the eyes of a mule. His boys' story 'For Name and Fame' appeared in serial form (as did some of the others) in *Every Boy's Annual* of 1886.

Henty prided himself on his military knowledge and yet, despite his hobby of yachting, seems as oddly reticent about describing sea campaigns as he is ready to write up military ones. In 1899, however, in the September issue of *Chambers's Journal*, his 'Torpedo-Boat 240, A Tale of the Naval Manoeuvres' appeared. Possibly the ageing Henty felt overshadowed by Kipling whose short and immensely readable 'A Fleet in Being' (notes of two trips with the Channel Squadron) had appeared the previous year.

The following are a few reviews of Henty books at the time when he had become an institution. From the 'Literary News and Books to be Read' section of the *Navy and Army Illustrated* of 16 December 1899, comes the following:

Mr Henty is certainly an astonishing man. For more years than I care to remember he has been pouring forth stories of adventure which have won him world-wide repute, and there is no falling off either in the quality or the freshness of the five volumes—if there are not more—which appear from his pen this Christmas. There is something of the prig in his heroes, perhaps, and behind his glowing pages the schoolmaster lies hid; but he is such a skilful contriver that these points are rarely discerned by his readers. He surveys the world from China to Peru . . .

On this occasion the five books reviewed were: *Won by the Sword*, *The Lion of the North*, *No Surrender!*, *A Roving Commission*, and *In Times of Peril*, although two of the five (*The Lion of the North* and *In Times of Peril*) were reissues. The critic also mentioned two other books, *Out on the Pampas* and *Yule Tide Yarns* (short stories), so that clearly Blackie's were cashing in on the Christmas trade with old editions as well as bringing out Henty's annual trio of new stories.

Henty's books were regularly reviewed in *Review of Reviews*— for example, after the appearance of *Condemned as a Nihilist* in 1892:

Wherever English is spoken one imagines that Mr. Henty's name is known. One cannot enter a schoolroom or look at a boy's bookshelf without seeing half-a-dozen of his familiar volumes. Now that Kingston is gone and Captain Marryat is never read—and more's the pity—Mr. Henty is no doubt the most successful writer for boys, and the one to whose new volumes they look forward every Christmas with most pleasure. Broadly, there are two classes of writers for boys: those who write a story with no intent to amuse, and those who write a story in which the plot is subservient to the moral. To neither of these classes does Mr. Henty belong. If his stories have any moral at all beyond the teaching of self-reliance, honesty and uprightness, we have not been able to discover it. He is satisfied with writing an exciting story, which he usually pitches in some period or country which will enable him to impart a little historical knowledge in a way that will not offend his readers—and boys are the most unforgiving of critics. This year Mr. Henty has chosen Russia as the scene of one of his yarns and a wonderfully exciting story it is.

A month later the same reviewer is back with a heading 'Two New Hentys', and is far from happy about the speed of production. The two new books are *Beric the Briton* and *In Greek Waters*. The latter is accorded only a few lines and is not well thought of.

A year later the following review appeared:

Last month we noticed what we thought the best of the three stories Mr. Henty has put forth this autumn. The two that remain, however, are very good, and show a deservedly popular author almost at his finest. *Through the Sikh War* is a tale of the

conquest of the Punjab, and deals with the prolonged struggle
which the British had to carry on before they could make sure of
maintaining their ascendancy in India. Of course Mr. Henty's
hero—he has the good luck to have an uncle the Governor, under
a native Prince, of a state in the Punjab—goes through the thick
of all the fighting and covers himself with honours, and equally of
course, Mr. Henty succeeds in imparting in an exceedingly un-
obtrusive and inoffensive way a deal of historical information in
the course of his narrative . . . Mr. Henty's other book—a shilling
cheaper, as usual—is *A Jacobite Exile*, and narrates the adventures
of a young English lad, whose father, denounced as a Royalist and
a plotter against the Elector, has to flee England, taking his son
with him. They make their way to Sweden; there the son enters
the foreign legion under Charles XII of Sweden and sees a deal
of fighting against the Russians and Poles.

One of the few things Henty might be said to sermonize against
in his books is drink, at least spirits. Henty himself smoked all day
as he worked and believed that smoking was not injurious provided
it was started after the age of twenty-one. He drank claret and water
with both lunch and dinner and thought beer could be bad only if
it affected the liver. He wanted to see the tax on spirits raised ten-
fold, and he said in 1882:

A glass of spirits and water may do no harm, but there is such a
tendency upon the part of those who use them to increase the
dose, and the end is, in that case, destruction to mind and body.

In his book *Twenty Years Ago—A Book of Anecdote*, published in
1905, Edmund Downey, who knew him, has a number of stories to
tell of Henty. He says that Henty managed to live in London on 16s.
a week in his young days and that the failure of the magazine, *Union-
Jack*, was a considerable blow to him. He it was who suggested that
Henty should use an amanuensis. Most amusing of his stories,
however, was his description of Henty at the time of the battle of
Majuba Hill:

Henty was the most Imperialist of all the Imperialists I ever
encountered. I remember well the day when the news of Majuba
Hill reached London. Henty appeared at Catherine Street a
little later than his usual hour.

'Have you heard this awful news?' he asked me as he arrived in the office. And then the big man burst into tears.

'The disgrace can never be wiped out,' he blubbered. 'Never! Never!'

There is an interesting reference to Henty by H. M. Hyndman in his biography of Clemenceau. This time the subject is the Dreyfus Affair:

Henty was a thorough-going Tory, but he had no doubt that Dreyfus was a terribly ill-used man and the victim of a foul plot—until he went over to France to watch the re-trial by court martial at Rennes. He returned in a quite different frame of mind. He knew I was entirely favourable to Dreyfus, as he himself had been when he crossed the Channel. Meeting him by accident I asked him his opinion: 'All I can tell you, Hyndman, is that I watched the man carefully throughout and he made a very bad impression upon me indeed. The longer I looked at him the worse I felt about him. I don't deny for a moment that his first trial was abominably conducted and that he was entitled to fair play. I daresay I may be all wrong . . . the weight of the evidence might have overborne me as a juryman. But, as it was, I felt that if I myself had been one of the jury I should have given a verdict against him. The man looked and spoke like a spy, and if he isn't a spy,' Henty went on in his impulsive way, 'I'll be damned if he oughtn't to be one'. That, of course, is simply the statement of an impressionable Englishman, who, however, understood what was going on.

Hyndman's account gives a revealing picture of Henty: honest in his instincts, wanting to be fairminded, ready to give way to his prejudices, impulsive and generous. Henty had many faults and towards the end of his life, apart from becoming something of a recluse, and embittered at that, had probably also developed into a bore. Of all his qualities it was, perhaps, his generosity and warmth that most endeared him to his contemporaries. Speaking of the Savage Club, which he adorned for many years, Henty said:

It comes home to me how warm is the feeling which the members of the Club cherish for each other, that the Savage is not a mere meeting place of brain-workers and kindred professionals, but a gathering of men who have a real earnest friendship, in many cases an almost brotherly affection for each other.

But, despite many anecdotes about his life, Henty remains something of an enigma. He had many public friends and yet his somewhat forbidding persona seemed to keep them at a distance and none of the accounts of him penetrates the shell—war correspondent, boys' writer extraordinary, clubman, bluff commanding figure of decided views—that he so successfully maintained to the world and sheltered behind. In the end, despite his many qualities, it is as though he became one of his own boy heroes: a successful adventurer who early establishes the mould from which he never afterwards departs. He is a figure of the stage; and he is also rather flat.

PART TWO

Attitudes and Techniques

CHAPTER THREE

Heroes and Techniques

THE MOULD OF his heroes was the vehicle which Henty used to convey the moral content of his stories. He early established the type—manly, straightforward, could give and take punishment (taking without complaint although more usually he seemed to be giving it), fearless, never lying, resourceful. Henty had certain obsessions and these are apparent after studying half a dozen of his stories. As a boy he had been sickly but, having trained himself in a number of sports and learnt to box, he grew into a large and powerful man. His youthful heroes almost always develop strong physiques: they usually learn to box and this enables them to defeat bigger and older opponents. Gentility was another Henty obsession and though occasionally his heroes come from—almost—working-class backgrounds there is always something special about them. Normally they are from sound middle-class families; sometimes from the gentry. Whatever their starting point improvement is the objective: of fortune and status.

In *The Young Buglers*, an early Henty, the typical pattern is set. Two brothers are at Eton when the story begins; their father is swindled out of his fortune and so the family falls on hard times. They run away and enlist as buglers in their uncle's old regiment. The officers soon recognize who they are—Henty was a snob about family and public schools and several times makes the point that the boys had been at Eton—and it therefore does not matter that they are also buglers for a time. Tom, the elder brother, has a fight with a much bigger bugler and wins and the boys become 'general favourites', a familiar Henty phrase attached to nearly all his heroes. They are off to Portugal for the Peninsular War and after the battle of Talavera they are promoted ensigns so are once more among their own officer-class friends.

Resourcefulness soon brings a Henty hero to the fore so that, often protesting, he assumes command. In *Under Drake's Flag* when the hero Ned and another boy, Tom, are shipwrecked in Patagonia, Tom concedes the leadership to Ned:

'Gerald told me he always relied upon you, and found you always right; you may be sure that I will do the same . . .'

'Well, my first order is,' Ned said laughing, 'that we each . . .'

and from then on Ned is in command. Later when Tom asks Ned a question the didactic hero replies: 'There can be no doubt that the natives make a sort of glue . . .'

Resourcefulness is, possibly, the most important characteristic of all for a Henty hero: it does not matter what education or background he may have he can always turn his hand to anything, and boys of sixteen see at once the strategic importance of points that apparently escape many older and more experienced campaigners. Typical of this strategic ability is the way in which Malcolm, the hero of *The Lion of the North* ('a Tale of the Thirty Years War'), rides into a village and promises to help the peasants defend it against marauding bands: 'I want the rest to bring mattocks and shovels and to accompany me along the road. There is one spot which I marked as I came along as being specially suited for defence.'

In most stories the physique of the hero and, for example, his growth from a fifteen-year-old at the beginning into a powerful broad-shouldered young man at the end will be described or his muscularity alluded to in some other way. Thus when young Malchus, the hero of *The Young Carthaginian*, is taken prisoner, 'Scipio, accustomed to estimate men, could not but admire the calm and haughty self-possession of his young prisoner. His eye fell with approval upon his active and sinewy figure, and the knotted muscles of his arms and legs.'

In *The Lion of St Mark* ('A Story of Venice in the Fourteenth Century') Polani, the benefactor of Francis, the hero, talks of the boy as Henty would describe all his heroes: 'But he is an excellent lad nevertheless, a true, honest, brave lad, with a little of the bluffness that they say all his nation possess, but with a heart of gold, unless I am greatly mistaken.'

This same hero later displays another less likeable Henty quality, that of superiority: 'Francis smiled quietly at the bigoted hatred which the captain bore the Genoese, but thought it useless to argue with him.' Back from his adventures, in the Polani household again,

Francis is taken to task by Maria, the elder of the Polani girls, for his inability to pay compliments, but Francis bluffly asserts he thinks to do so is a silly business.

The hero of *The Lion of St Mark* is a paragon. Having by a daring and clever exploit recaptured a merchant vessel from pirates Francis says of his achievement, 'It was just a happy idea', so illustrating another hero characteristic, modesty. Like most Henty heroes Francis is a prig. Thus he reproves his Venetian friend, Matteo, for going to a reception and enjoying himself:

'Talking about what, Matteo?'
'The heat, and the music, and the costumes, and the last bit of scandal at the Piazza.'
'I don't call that talk, I call it chatter. And now, Matteo, I shall leave you to your own devices, for I am going to turn in and get a sleep for a few hours.'

Such a friend may be splendid in a crisis; he can hardly be much fun as a companion.

Francis, indeed, is a rich example of a Henty hero possessed of all the most tedious attributes of his kind. He lectures and, when he and Matteo are captives in the hold of a vessel and begin cutting themselves out, he says: 'You will find, Matteo, that your arms will ache so that you cannot hold them up before the end of three hours . . .'

Henty also considered it important to establish that his heroes were average as far as brains were concerned despite their resourcefulness. In *One of the 28th* ('A Tale of Waterloo'), for example, the vicar describes the hero, Ralph: 'He is evidently a straightforward, manly lad. I don't mean to say that he has any exceptional amount of brains, or is likely to set the Thames on fire; but if he comes into the Penfold property that will not be of much importance.'

Contrasts between English and French habits emphasize the quality of manliness so essential to all Henty heroes. At one point in *One of the 28th* Ralph is picked up by a French privateer and befriended by an English-speaking French sailor:

Jacques laughed good-temperedly. 'There would be nothing to be ashamed of. We are not like you cold English! A Frenchman laughs and sings when he is pleased and cries when he is sorry. Why shouldn't he?'

'Oh, I can't tell you why,' Ralph replied, 'only we don't do it. I don't say I shouldn't holloa out if I were hurt very much, though I should try my best not to; but I feel sure I shouldn't cry like a great baby. Why, what would be the good of that?'

Jacques shrugs and gives an example of French boys fighting and pulling each other's hair and crying—but continuing to fight. His efforts at educating Ralph do not get him far.

'Pulling each other's hair!' Ralph repeated contemptuously. 'They ought to have been ashamed of themselves, both of them. I don't call that fighting at all. I should call it disgusting. Why, in England even girls would hardly pull each other's hair . . . If that's the way French boys fight, no wonder our soldiers and sailors . . .'

But here discretion takes over.

Another Ned is the hero of *By Pike and Dyke* ('A Tale of the Rise of the Dutch Republic'); he becomes a confidant of the Prince of Orange and at one point gives a rousing speech to the citizens of Haarlem, so strengthening their resolve to continue the fight. Ned, who is all of seventeen by this time, then turns and says modestly to a senior soldier: 'I shall look to you, sir, for your aid and assistance. The prince is pleased to have a good opinion of me; but I am young, and shall find the responsibility a very heavy one, and can only hope to maintain my authority by the aid of your assistance.'

Apart from the tautology—his work suffered from the fact that he dictated his stories and did not look at the results before they went to the publishers—Henty was often in difficulty over the problem of modesty. He makes the point many times that his heroes are—and must be—modest. At the same time it is essential to reveal the extent of their achievements, and sometimes the only person who can do this is the hero himself. Thus when this same Ned returns to England, sick, but decked in finery, he has to explain his appearance to his mother: 'Indeed I think I am very moderate in not decking myself out with the two gold chains I have—the one a present from his highness, the other from the city of Alkmaar—to say nothing of the watch set with jewels that the prince gave me on leaving.'

Almost without exception Henty's heroes are over-earnest young men with little sense of humour and though the author often begins his stories by describing them as full of fun and always into scrapes

—a device to obtain the sympathy of his young readership—thereafter, once the main action of the story gets underway, they become sober, far-sighted, earnest and wise before their time.

Another standby in Henty's books is boxing and the advantages of a straight left. Godfrey, the hero of *Condemned as a Nihilist* ('The Story of Escape from Siberia'), fights the prison bully in Siberia and knocks him down. His friend Mikail comes forward to intervene but: 'Let us alone, Mikail. This fellow has been a nuisance in the ward ever since I came. It is just as well that he should have a lesson. I shan't do him any harm. Just leave us alone for a minute or two; he won't want much more.'

Explaining his easy victory over a man twice his size Godfrey says:

That is the great point of boxing, Osip. One learns to keep cool, and to have one's wits about one; for anyone who loses his temper has but a poor chance indeed against another who keeps cool. Moreover a man who can box well will always keep his head in all times of danger and difficulty. It gives him nerve and self-confidence, and enables him at all times to protect the weak against the strong.

This same hero escapes down the river Ob; like all Henty heroes he is loquacious. He has a Russian, Luka, with him who simply shakes his head when he does not understand. Undeterred, Godfrey happily lectures his Russian companion about God, Russia or anything else he has on his mind. Luka, luckily perhaps, comprehends little of what Godfrey says. They eventually reach Norway and the Norwegians find it difficult to believe that Godfrey has indeed escaped from Siberia. He reassures them: 'There has been no great difficulty about it. We have kept near the coast, and have generally landed when bad weather came on. I have a gun, and with that and fishing there has been no difficulty about food . . .' At the end of this particular story Henty makes a point that applies to all his heroes: 'His spirits were as high and he was as full of fun as of old; but the experience he had gone through had strengthened his character, had given him self-reliance and confidence, and has, as his father and mother soon saw, had a very beneficial effect in forming his character.'

Henty heroes, however distant their period in time, possess the characteristics of Victorian school prefects of the better, all-round variety: 'The time passed quickly and pleasantly at Steyning. Wulf studied hard for three or four hours a day, looked after his tenants, hunted and hawked, doubled the number of his housecalls, and often rode over to the priory of an evening.' Thus the hero of *Wulf the Saxon* is a prodigy of unusual Saxon zeal.

There is a hypercritical piety about Henty heroes which can be nauseating, though it is, perhaps, doubtful that Henty recognized this characteristic. Gervaise, the hero of *A Knight of the White Cross* ('A Tale of the Siege of Rhodes'), is to be honoured for his exploits by the city of Genoa and expresses the wish that his friend Ralph could go in his place; when Ralph says he must simply put up with the honours that are to be showered upon him the pious Gervaise replies: 'If one were fighting for fame and honour, all that would be true enough; but members of an Order, whose sole object is to defend Christendom from the Moslems, should strive only to do their duty, and care nothing for such things as honour and glory.' Such an attitude does not prevent Gervaise reaping both honour and glory throughout the book. The more worldly Ralph answers Gervaise in good Victorian terms: 'Human nature is human nature, and I don't see any reason why one should despise honour and glory when they come to one in the course of duty.'

Henty heroes never put a foot wrong. In part, of course, this is a necessary device so that they can be appointed to the staff of Wolfe, Frederick the Great, Turenne or Wellington, so enabling the author to mix their doings with the history lesson and portrait of the great figure he wishes to put over in the particular book. In his later books Henty also makes his heroes noticeably more ruthless and machine-like, a reflection of both the author's own ability to turn out three such books every year and possibly of the bitterness he undoubtedly felt about social reactions to his second marriage. Thus, in *A Roving Commission* ('Through the Black Insurrection of Hayti'), published in 1900, he allows his hero to blow out the brains of an unconscious man who has attacked their hiding place, on the grounds that he dare not let him escape. The hero of *With Roberts to Pretoria* ('A Tale of the South African War') engineers the massacre of nine men—admittedly thieves—who break into a house. There is a cold efficiency about these later heroes. In *With the Allies to Pekin* ('A Story of the Relief of the Legations'), one of the worst Henty books, there is an unintentionally funny line when the hero rescues his young girl cousins from Boxers in a blazing building: 'It is all right, girls!' Rex cried. 'I am Rex, and I have come here to save you!'

This he duly does; he is accompanied by a faithful Chinese follower, Ah Lo. They fight some Boxers and by then the girls have clearly adopted a merciless spirit too: 'Oh, how could you do it, Rex? I am not sorry for the Boxers a bit, but it is wonderful that you two should have killed twelve of them in two minutes; I am sure the firing did not last longer than that.'

A really bad book may hold as great a fascination for the reader as a really good one. *Through Three Campaigns* has only one or two rivals for the distinction of being Henty's very worst book.* Its hero, Bullen, gets the V.C. for rescuing a brother officer under fire. Describing what he had done, this paragon says: 'When Blunt fell, it was the most natural thing in the world that I should go and pick him up, and I did so almost mechanically.' Indeed, it is the major criticism of almost all Henty's heroes that they act and react 'almost mechanically'.

As far as story is concerned, Henty may be described as a formula writer. Usually the story begins when the hero is aged fifteen or thereabouts and, because of the death of his father or some other family misfortune, is thrown on his own resources. He may join the army; he may have a letter of introduction to an old family friend; he may be sent for by an uncle. During the early stages of the book, perhaps while he is at school, there will be two or three adventures designed to establish the sturdy independence and openness of the hero; he will be a troublemaker but one who plays practical jokes and earns a thrashing for them, he will never do anything dishonourable. Then, using one of several devices, Henty gets his hero to the main scene of the story's action—Gibraltar during the siege, for example—and there he will soon enough be noticed by the commanding officer or some other high-ranking historical personage. From that point onwards Henty weaves the adventures of his hero into an account of the campaign he wishes to describe and, since the hero is usually attached—at least for a time—as an aide-de-camp or in some other capacity to someone such as Frederick the Great, this allows the author naturally and easily to present a portrait of the historic figure as well. During the course of his adventures the hero will be captured, and escape, at least once, often twice. He may be brought into the presence of a famous enemy; thus Malchus in *The Young Carthaginian* not only serves Hannibal, whose

---

* There certainly seems to be a fair consensus among members of the Henty Society about the awfulness of *Through Three Campaigns*.

exploits and character are described, but is brought into contact with Scipio as a prisoner. The hero also meets, and very often rescues from some peril, a girl, usually aged about fourteen at that point, who is clearly destined to be his wife—at the end of the book. She is likely to be an heiress, although most Henty heroes in any case gain substantial riches along the way as prize money, in the form of presents from rich potentates they serve or fortunes left by older men who 'adopt' them in the course of the narrative. There are variations but this is the pattern that Henty maintained through some eighty full-length boys' books.

Henty contrives to bring as many historic figures as possible into contact, however brief, with his heroes. In *The Young Franc-Tireurs*, about the Franco-Prussian war, for example, the two brothers carry a dangerous message into besieged Paris, meet Gambetta himself, escape from the city in a balloon. His heroes always have a plan for the most complicated situation; they usually appear to know much more than anyone else; and more often than not offer advice to the top people as to how things should be done —and their advice is followed.

The pattern may seem stereotyped but was successful and Henty stuck to it. At its best, when he got the mixture (of hero's adventures and historical account) right, the formula was an ideal vehicle for teaching history painlessly. At its worst, the formula degenerated into a series of devices to ensure that the hero was present first at one and then at another event of historical importance which the author wished to describe.

One Henty device is to make a character—perhaps a sailor— recount some of his experiences to the hero. Sometimes, fairly obviously, this is a device to fill up space—Henty's contract with Blackie's specified three books a year of up to 140,000 words each. Often, however, it is clear that Henty had good material which he felt was worth the telling and it was simply a question of inventing a reasonable excuse for inserting it in the story.

The most irritating of all Henty's techniques was a particular form of repetition he deemed essential, apparently, to ensure that his readers missed none of the hero's achievements. Thus the hero would carry out a brave deed and win recognition or promotion as a result. Back in the regiment his commanding officer will insist he describes what he did for the benefit of his admiring brother officers, so we are treated to the account for a second time. Later—

possibly the hero is being assigned to some especially dangerous duty—his commanding officer will explain to others for the third time the same exploit of the hero and on this occasion the reason for the repetition is to explain why the hero rather than someone else is being honoured or given a chance to distinguish himself. Whether avid Henty readers recognized such passages and skipped them or felt reinforced by the repetition of the hero's achievements is an open question.

The most important of all Henty's techniques was that of mixing history with adventures in such a way as to make it palatable to his young readers. In his preface to *The Young Buglers* ('A Tale of the Peninsular War') Henty says:

> I remember that, as a boy, I regarded any attempt to mix instruction with amusement as being as objectionable a practice as the administration of powder in jam; but I think that this feeling arose from the fact that in those days books contained a very small share of amusement and a very large share of instruction. I have endeavoured to avoid this . . .

This, indeed, was the secret of Henty's success and boys uninterested in history could still read one of his books as an adventure story, no doubt skipping the descriptions of battles or other set historical pieces when these occurred. At the end of the same preface Henty says: 'The military facts, with the names of generals and regiments, the dates and places, are all strictly accurate and anyone who has read with care the story of *The Young Buglers* could pass an examination as to the leading events of the Peninsular War.'

Henty prided himself upon his historical accuracy and one of the more tedious ways in which he brought this out in book after book was by giving long lists of all the regiments, the numbers and the names of officers who took part in a battle or campaign. Sometimes such lists cover pages; one of the snappier ones occurs in the story *In Freedom's Cause* ('A Story of Wallace and Bruce'). Before the battle of Bannockburn, he lists the commanders of the English army: 'Among the leaders of this great army were the Earls of Gloucester, Pembroke, Hereford and Angus, Lord Clifford, Sir John Comyn, Sir Henry Beaumont, Sir John Seagrave, Sir Edmund Morely, Sir Ingram de Umfraville, Sir Marmaduke de Twenge, and Sir Giles de Argentine, one of the most famous of the Continental knights.'

A Henty technique that provides some variation is that of having two heroes. Sometimes they are brothers as in *Jack Archer* or *Through Russian Snows*; or they are friends, as in *Orange and Green* which is set in Ireland at the time of the battle of the Boyne when one boy is Protestant and the other Catholic, or in *Friends Though Divided* when the two boys are on opposite sides in the Civil War.

The fathers of Henty's heroes must necessarily be disposed of early in his books; or, if permitted to live, they are curious recluse characters of weak or erratic dispositions who give a virtually free hand to their sons to go their own ways or organize and save the family fortunes.

The collapse of the family fortune was often the event which set the young hero off on his adventures; essentially Henty was writing for the rising middle classes and he so designed these family disasters that the young, comfortably-off boys who read the stories could feel the thrill of deprivation without the anxiety of want. Thus the scale of the middle-class disaster which engulfs the clergyman's family at the beginning of *With Roberts to Pretoria* is demonstrated by their proposed economies:

> I shall at once give notice to the coachman and gardener. The boy must be kept on. He can look after the pony, and do the rough work in the garden with the aid of a man hired for a day occasionally. One of the maids must, of course, go. We shall see how well we can manage, and I hope we shall be able to keep the other two.

The hero has to leave Rugby.

The need to explain everything precisely to his readers was clearly a didactic imperative with Henty. The result is not only lengthy and wordy conversations, in which his heroes explain what they have done, how and why, but also, not infrequently, long soliloquies by the heroes when, for example, in captivity, as they work out a method of escape.

The sheer volume of important historic figures a hero will meet in the course of a story is the result of the most blatant of all Henty techniques as he shifts his hero around like a pawn on a chessboard. In *A Jacobite Exile*, for example, the hero Charlie meets and is befriended by Charles XII of Sweden, the Czar Peter of Russia, and the Duke of Marlborough, as well as being presented to Queen Anne. He encounters a host of minor historical characters as well.

One of Henty's dilemmas arises out of the difficulty he faces in making his characters both heroic and ordinary. On the one hand, his heroes will often pass through an impossible series of adventures in which they constantly distinguish themselves. On the other, part of the author's purpose is to portray boys or young men who are all of a pattern, possessing the identical characteristics needed for a typical administrator or soldier in the Empire. Thus, back with the pious Gervaise (from *A Knight of the White Cross*): he suspects a Greek of being a spy and his friend, Ralph, gets annoyed with him and says tartly: 'Such ideas do not so much as occur to them, and I must say that I think the sooner you fall into the ways of other people the better.' Real heroes do not conform; Henty was painting an ideal.

The most successful Henty technique of all was to turn the hero of any time or place into a late Victorian public schoolboy prefect off to fight for the Empire, with whom his readers could instantly identify.

Henty's style is clear and straightforward; it is also repetitive and on the whole pedestrian. In his first half a dozen books he is searching for the pattern that was later to become his hallmark and is still influenced by the more didactic 'preaching' approach which characterized so much of the pre-Henty period writing for children. Henty is never very happy recreating medieval or earlier language. In *St. George for England* ('A Tale of Cressy and Poitiers'), for example, he starts using language such as the following: 'Here I will leave you, and will one of these days return to inquire if your health has taken ought of harm by the rough buffetting of the storm of yester-even.' Once he has contributed a few pages of such clumsy speech, however, Henty usually gets on with the story.

Sometimes he descends to a banal level of explanation:

> The shouts of satisfaction and the departure of forty or fifty men at full speed in various directions did not pass unnoticed by the garrison of the tower.
> 'They have got a plan of some sort,' Malcolm said . . .

And sometimes he is guilty of glaring anachronisms which should certainly have been spotted at the proof-reading stage and result from his habit of dictating as many as seven thousand words in a day's sitting. In *The Dragon and the Raven* ('Or The Days of King Alfred'), for example, he says of the battle order: 'On his right were the men of Somerset and Hants; on the left those of Wilts, Dorset, and Devon.'

Henty's forays into Biblical-style language are heavy-handed. He does this in *For The Temple* ('A Tale of the Fall of Jerusalem'):

> 'We are in God's hands, John,' she said with the quiet resignation of her race. 'He can save us if He will; let us pray to Him.'

While in *The Cat of Bubastes* ('A Tale of Ancient Egypt') he at once establishes an Israelite-Jewish character by such speech as the following:

> 'What is it?' he exclaimed as Jethro entered. 'Has the God of our fathers again smitten me in my old age, and taken from me my pet lamb? I heard her cry, but my limbs have lost their power, and I could not rise to come to her aid.'

Simple mistakes of language appear, though not often, and clearly result from Henty using an amanuensis to whom he dictated. Thus in *A Knight of the White Cross* Gervaise feels 'no hilarity', instead of exhilaration, at his promotion.

Won by the Sword ('A Tale of the Thirty Years' War') is set in France in the time of Mazarin and is clearly derived in part from Dumas' *Twenty Years After*; it is a rattling good period piece yarn more than a history, and what history there is never obtrudes. It also contains one of the most glaring of Henty's anachronisms. The hero, a young Scot called Hector, is describing to two French officers the qualities he requires in the man he is trying to find to serve as a lackey. One of the officers then says: 'And I suppose that this Admirable Crichton of whom you are in search must be sober, honest and truthful.'

Henty's dialogue is often unintentionally funny. When Desmond, the hero of *In The Irish Brigade* ('A Tale of the War in Flanders and Spain') hears a woman's cry for help and scales a twelve-foot wall into a private garden to investigate, he is challenged, so:

> 'Stop!' Desmond cried in a loud voice. 'I am an officer of O'Brien's regiment of foot. I heard a scream and a woman's cry for help, and, fearing that foul play was going on, I made my entry here.'

Needless to say he then rescues an heiress.

In some of his last books—*With the Allies to Pekin* is an excellent example—Henty had become lazy, so that the devices whereby he ensures that his hero moves rapidly from one scene of action to another in order that he may describe them all become increasingly threadbare and strain credulity. *By Conduct and Courage*, published posthumously, again has an 'Admirable Crichton' popping up. At the end, indeed, Henty had become a sort of machine and sometimes a rather careless and bored one.

Henty's heroes are more or less uniformly dull: virtuous and heroic yet destined to be bores in the long twilight of their lives, for with few exceptions their adventures are over by the age of twenty-five or so and they settle to a life of respectable married bliss as pillars of the local establishment. Henty compensates for these boring fellows by what is often his best device: the follower. These characters are always of lower social origins; sometimes they are faithful natives and they act as servants and friends. They are often vested by Henty with greater character than their masters possess, almost as though he is compensating for the necessity to turn out stereotypes to fill the hero roles.

The variety of these followers is wide. Sam, a negro soldier in *The Young Buglers*, who is made much good-humoured fun of in the regiment, becomes the devoted servant of the two boys who early in the story save his life. In *The Cornet of Horse* Rupert is followed to the Marlborough Wars by Hugh Parsons from his estate. In London the two boys determine their roles:

'Not a lackey, perhaps, but a sort of confidential retainer. That will be best, Master Rupert, in every way.'

Rupert was silent for a moment.

'Well, Hugh, perhaps that would be best; but you must remember that whatever we are before others, we are always friends when we are alone.'

'Very well,' Hugh said, 'that is understood; but you know that alone or before others, I shall always be your faithful servant.'

Thus—and in many other stories—position, class and loyalty are suitably established.

Often, of course, it is a faithful native. Thus in *A Final Reckoning* ('A Tale of Bush Life in Australia') Reuben the hero has an Aborigine follower: 'The native, Jim, was still with him. He had become greatly attached to his master, and his fidelity and devotion had been of the greatest service to him, and go where he would the black was always at his heels.'

In *The Bravest of the Brave* ('With Peterborough in Spain') the hero, Jack Stilwell, has an old soldier as his follower, a sergeant who is clearly a rogue and takes in the hero throughout the story. At the end Jack describes him to Peterborough as 'a willing and faithful soldier of the queen, and really a worthy fellow', to which the earl replies: 'He is evidently an arrant old scamp, Stilwell. Still, as long as we recruit our army as we do, we cannot look for morality as well as bravery, and I dare say your fellow is no worse than the rest.'

One of the best such characters is Pierre, the follower of Philip, the hero of *St Bartholomew's Eve* ('A Tale of the Huguenot Wars'). There is an excellent illustration which shows Philip eyeing his servant-to-be from a doorway, and while Philip looks like a pious prefect Pierre is a down-at-heel rogue. Pierre gets his master out of more than one scrape, showing greater quickness and intelligence in the process, and Henty, one feels, sometimes allowed himself to have a little fun—not much—with such characters since they were not being put forward as models.

In *Wulf the Saxon*, the hero Wulf is followed by one Osgod, the son of an armourer and a mighty fighter. He is one of Henty's more inspired inventions: big, loutish, lazy, kind, and eats like a horse. All he wants is faithfully to serve his master and fight; he does both throughout the book.

It is difficult to determine whether the contrasts Henty sometimes draws between his manly, priggish heroes and their more human followers is deliberate humour on the part of an author sometimes bored with the piety of his main characters or whether he saw it this way at all. In *Won by the Sword*, Paolo (the Admirable Crichton whom the hero Hector eventually engages as his servant) turns out to be far cleverer and more interesting than his master. The two youths have to take a message into the citadel of Turin during the siege; this entails several swims through moats or icy rivers. To the indomitable Hector, of course, they are nothing and when poor Paolo shivers at the prospect of yet another swim—by then they are in the middle of a blinding snowstorm—Hector admonishes him with the sturdy nonchalance expected of a Victorian public schoolboy captain of games: 'Nonsense! One cold bath more or less makes no difference now.'

However interesting these followers may be they always know their place. Roper, who is the follower of Arthur, the hero of *With*

the British Legion ('A Story of the Carlist Wars'), is often told by his
master that he would like to push him forward until Roper discovers
that one day Arthur will return to England to become a squire.
Arthur offers to give him a farm on his estate.

> That is all right, sir. We were friends together for a time, but I
> was in my right position and you were not. That, of course, was
> soon put right, and we have stood ever since in the proper
> relation towards each other. I am only too glad to work for you,
> and now you have put me in for a very good thing.

The disguises to which Henty's heroes frequently resort often
appear ludicrous to adult eyes yet were a necessary part of his stories
and acceptable if not entirely credible, perhaps, to his young
readers. Some are hard to take: the two boys in *The Young Franc-
Tireurs*, for example, aged seventeen and fifteen, disguise themselves
as a Jewish father and son (peddlers) and so pass through the Prussian
lines into besieged Paris. In the Indian stories dyes are produced at
the drop of a hat and the hero will be off in his stains and turban as a
Sikh to pass effortlessly among the enemy. And once, at least, even
Henty could not take his own disguise and in *With the British
Legion* he makes half of Arthur's false moustache come off when the
hero is attending a ball in the Carlist lines. Arthur is obliged to run
for his life.

There is plenty of instruction in Henty's stories but it is never
overpowering or obtrusive and fits well enough into the stage the
story has by then reached. In the early novels the teaching is more
obvious. Thus in *Out on the Pampas* ('The Young Settlers'), which
was Henty's first boys' book, he says, for example: 'The word camp
in the Pampas means station or property; it is a corruption of the
Spanish word *campos*, literally plains or meadows'; or, 'The way in
which adobe or mud houses are constructed is as follows . . .'
Indeed this book is full of instruction and one chapter entitled
'Quiet Times' describes how to cultivate tobacco, how to grow sugar
cane and then turn it into sugar. In later books the instruction is
slipped in more casually. Thus in *Condemned as a Nihilist*, which
contains magnificent descriptions of Siberia and the winter, including the break-up of the ice on the river when the spring comes,
the simple statement, 'It is not the sun or the rain that breaks up the
ice, but the rise of the river from the snow melting a thousand
miles higher up,' is inserted.

Henty had a love for the sea, although surprisingly few of his novels take a great sea captain as the historical figure. The sea, none the less, features in almost every book he wrote. In some cases the young hero is brought up by the sea and his first adventure, perhaps, is in a fishing boat during a storm. Almost all Henty's heroes go abroad for their main adventures and on the voyage out—to Spain for the Peninsular War, to Africa or India—there is at least one chapter and sometimes several devoted to the voyage, a storm, a brush with privateers. Smuggling off the English coast features quite prominently in a number of books and Henty treats this as an acceptable occupation, certainly in the stories of eighteenth- or nineteenth-century Britain. The adventure in a boat off the Gold Coast which forms part of *By Sheer Pluck* was based upon Henty's own journey in a ramshackle craft with H. M. Stanley during Wolseley's campaign in 1873. The sea appeared in Henty's books as part of the heritage of England or Britain which he so wanted to depict to his readers; it also appeared because he loved it himself and wanted to write about it. Some of his best descriptive passages are of the sea, usually in a storm.

In *A Final Reckoning* ('A Tale of Bush Life in Australia') a substantial part of the story is concerned with the journey out to Australia and in the course of it Henty describes being in the eye of the storm:

> 'Look up!' Bill said to Reuben; 'you may be at sea fifty years and never see that again.'
>
> Reuben looked up. Immediately overhead was a small circle of blue sky round and round whose edge the edging cloud seemed to be circling with extreme velocity. The light seemed to pierce straight down on to the vessel, and she stood pale and white while all round her a pitchy blackness seemed to prevail.
>
> 'We are in the eye of the storm, my lad. Here it comes. Now, hold on for your life.'

Henty's endings are all the same. Writing for boys aged eleven to fourteen, he had to ensure they could identify with the hero; the result was a central character who usually started the story aged about fifteen and ended it aged, perhaps, twenty-five. Henty then had to tidy up: the result was that he had to marry the hero off, see he had a fortune and explain in a line or two how he spent the rest of his life.

It is possibly one of the most annoying aspects of Henty stories that all his heroes end up both rich and honoured. He set the pattern in his first book, *Out on the Pampas*, when after six years the Hardy family has done so well that the father can afford to return home leaving the boys to manage the estate which is the largest and most prosperous in the area. Astonishingly, perhaps, the last two pages of this story are taken up with financial calculations on the part of Mr. Hardy as to the value of the estate, how much he can take out of it each year, how much the boys can have. Henty was obviously much concerned with money for most of his life; he never lets the subject obtrude itself into a story quite so blatantly again. At the very end of *Out on the Pampas* Mr. Hardy finishes his calculations as follows:

'You, with care, can certainly save £5,000 each in the ten years, and will receive another £10,000 each as your share of the estate. You will consequently, boys, at the age of thirty-one and thirty-two, be able to settle down in England in very comfortable circumstances. Your sisters will of course be provided for out of my share. Do you approve of my plans?'

The boys warmly expressed their satisfaction at the plan, and their gratitude to their father for his intentions.

And so things were carried out.

This was the first novel. In almost all the later ones the boys would make their own fortunes rather than be dependent upon their father.

Occasionally the heroes do not finish with a fortune but exchange their adventures for a career. Thus at the end of *The Young Franc-Tireurs* (another early story) the two brothers return to their parents at Dijon and their father argues that they have done all that honour requires; the cause is lost, it would be foolish to go on fighting. 'I agree with you altogether, papa,' Ralph said. 'I have seen and had quite enough fighting for my lifetime.' They apply for sick leave and stay at home thereafter; later they go to London and Ralph joins the artillery while Percy studies at the bar.

These are early stories. The more familiar type of ending was established in *The Cornet of Horse*. In this case the hero is made a colonel by Marlborough on the field after the battle of Malplaquet. He also accepts—since to refuse would cause pain—a large cheque from a Dutch merchant friend he has made. Then Rupert returns home and marries. 'Had Rupert desired it, he could have been raised to the peerage, but he preferred remaining one of the wealthiest private gentlemen in England.' This becomes the more or less stock ending.

Another important ingredient of Henty's endings is that of keeping together the participants in the story: thus the faithful followers always settle with their masters so that they can tell the children and grandchildren of the hero's adventures when 'he was a Cornet of Horse' or whatever. At the end of *Under Drake's Flag*, for example, the friends settle in their native Devon and meet in each other's houses at least four times a year: 'Upon all these occasions stories were told at great length, and their children, grandchildren, and great-grandchildren, for all lived to see these growing up, were never tired of listening to tales of the Spanish Main.' Perhaps the children, grandchildren and great-grandchildren were just being polite.

All Henty heroes go through three stages. At first they are youngsters: full of fun, brave, dashing, troublemakers but of the right manly kind. Then they become involved in their chief historical adventure and their boyish qualities are tempered by the responsibilities of leadership and fighting in some guise for England or Empire. At the end they return home to settle down and become pillars of the establishment and they do this whether as ancient Britons in the time of Rome, in Saxon times, under Queen Elizabeth I or in the eighteenth and nineteenth centuries as returning soldiers of fortune. The height of Henty's ambition for his young heroes is that they come back to England to marry and become comfortably-off squires, M.P.s should they wish and undoubtedly Tories; moreover, judging by the number of stories which end with children, grandchildren, friends or followers gathering year after year to hear their early adventures, prize bores.

CHAPTER FOUR

Morality: Religion—Drink—Girls

HENTY BROKE WITH the earlier tradition of long sermons in his boys' books, hence his great popularity, yet he had a clear moral purpose as extracts from reviews demonstrate. A sentence from a review of *Facing Death* which appeared in the *Standard*, for example, reads: 'If any father, godfather, clergyman, or school-master is on the look-out for a good book to give as a present to a boy who is worth his salt, this is the book we would recommend.' While a review of *By Sheer Pluck* in the *Christian Leader* said: 'Morally, the book is everything that could be desired, setting before the boys a bright and bracing ideal of the English gentleman.'

Henty's religion was of the broad Anglican variety. He was certainly not bigoted, as his reflections upon the differences between Protestantism and Catholicism, which occur in a number of his books, reveal. Sometimes he makes mild fun of religion or at least its more entrenched aspects, and in some books the subject hardly occurs at all. He favoured muscular Christianity with the emphasis, in terms of his own life and writings, upon the muscle rather than the Christianity.

In most Henty stories there may appear a brief mention of religion in such a way that it was assumed to be a matter of course. In *The Young Franc-Tireurs*, for example, the two Barclay brothers have to swim across the icy Seine to get into Paris during the siege: 'The boys knelt down together, and asked for protection through the peril which they were about to encounter; a few minutes later they rose, grasped each other's hand, and then . . .' Or, in *Under Drake's Flag*, when two boys are shipwrecked upon a Spanish island Henty pays his customary tribute to God: 'One of the first thoughts of the boys upon fairly recovering themselves was to kneel down and thank God for having preserved their lives . . .'

In the same book the two boys later fall into the hands of the

Inquisition, and Henty says: 'By the boys, however, brought up in England, which at that time was bitterly and even fiercely anti-Catholic—a state of things which naturally followed the doings in the reign of Queen Mary, and the threatening aspect maintained by Spain towards this country—popery was held in utter abhorrence . . .' Earlier in the text Henty made a typical nineteenth-century comment: 'Nowadays we believe—at least all right-minded men believe—that there is good in all creeds, and that it would be rash indeed to condemn men who act to the best of their lights, even though those lights may not be their own.'

The Dragon and the Raven is set in the days of King Alfred and part of the story concerns the siege of Paris by the Northmen. Here Henty recounts with a certain relish a number of the so-called miracles of St. Germain that helped save the city, and finishes with the laconic statement: 'The Abbé D'Abbon vouches for these miracles on the part of St. Germain in defence of his faithful city.' At the end of this story the hero, Edmund, marries Freda who is a Dane:

> 'I trust, Freda,' Edmund said to her after a while, 'that you have thought of the talk we had about religion, and that you will forsake the barbarous gods of your people and become a Christian, as so many of your people have done in England, and that you will be wedded to me not in the rude way of the Danes, but in a Christian church,'

There is a distinct flavour of Victorian imperial-missionary zeal about this little speech.

In his preface to *Orange and Green*, Henty says:

> The subject of Ireland is one which has for some years been a very prominent one, and is likely, I fear, for some time yet to occupy a large share of public attention . . . The discontent manifested in the troubles of recent years has had its root in an older sense of grievance, for which there was, unhappily, only too abundant reason.

That was written in 1888. When he mentions religion in the story Henty argues for tolerance, thus: 'After all, we believe all the same important things; and as to others, what does it matter, provided we all do our best in the way that seems right to us?' At the end of this story the young hero who is Catholic marries a Protestant girl and again Henty makes his point about tolerance:

> 'That is just my view,' Mrs. Conyers agreed. 'The differences between the creeds are political rather than religious, and in any case I consider that when neither of the parties is bigoted, the chances of happiness are greater in the case where the man is a Catholic and the woman a Protestant than in the opposite case.'

Orange and Green is one of Henty's dual hero books: the two boys are drawn one from an older established Catholic family and the other from the recently Cromwellian planted Protestant families; during the war they fight in opposing armies yet remain friends throughout and by their conduct censure the excesses of both sides.

In *The Cat of Bubastes*, set in ancient Egypt, the High Priest has come to doubt the many Egyptian gods and is a secret monotheist. When the crisis of the story comes he explains his belief to his son who has become the friend of Amuba, the hero. As he reveals his doubts about the pantheon of animal gods of the Egyptians he sounds like a sensible parson at work. It is a little much, however, then to be told of the two boys:

> But there was in addition their own inward conviction of the truth of his theory. It appealed at once to their heads and hearts. It satisfied all their longing and annihilated their doubts and difficulties; cleared away at once the pantheon of strange and fantastic figures that had been a source of doubting amusement to Amuba, and of bewilderment to Chebron.

This sounds too much like confirmation.

Henty repeatedly makes a plea for religious tolerance and, since a number of his stories concern Spain at the height of her power, he has a good deal to say of Catholicism. Thus in *By Right of Conquest* ('With Cortez in Mexico') the hero, Roger, reflects:

> What should we think at home if an Indian were to arrive, and to try and teach us that our God was a false one? Why, he would be burnt at the stake in no time. And one cannot expect that these Indians would be more patient in such a matter than we should. When the Spaniards come they will doubtless overthrow their gods, and force them to be Christians, just as they have the peoples in the islands.

Henty's broadness, indeed, comes out later in this same story when he excuses his hero's ignorance of Aztec religion:

> All this, however, was unknown to Roger at the time; he saw the dark side of their religion only, and was ignorant that there underlay it a system which, in point of morality, love of order and method, and a broad charity, was in no way inferior to that practised among Christian nations.

Narrow church proselytizers of the time must have had their doubts about Henty.

A doubly ironical passage occurs in *Under Drake's Flag*. Henty is being sarcastic about missionary zeal, on this occasion at the expense of the Catholics. He makes his point in the context of Portuguese imperial methods, although almost certainly failing to see that the same kind of criticism could be similarly made at the expense of his beloved British Empire. A priest is attempting the mass conversion to Catholicism of some defeated natives and after a two-hour harangue, which is entirely in Portuguese and not understood by the natives at all, the governor gives a short, loose and succinct translation:

> There is only one God. These idols of yours are helpless and useless. We have brought ashore those from your war canoes, which my men will now proceed to burn, and you will see that your gods will be unable to help themselves. Indeed, they are not gods, and have no power. God is good and hates wickedness. All men are wicked. Therefore He would hate all men; but He has sent His Son down, and for His sake pardons all who believe in Him. Now, if you believe in Him as I tell you, you will be pardoned both by us and by God. If you do not believe, we shall kill you all and you will be punished eternally. Now you have the choice what to do.
>
> The matter thus pithily put did not require much consideration . . .

A mass conversion follows.

Henty's attitude towards religion is best summed up when in *A March on London* ('Being A Story of Wat Tyler's Insurrection)' he makes a knight say: 'Surely we have had experience enough to see that solid advantages are not to be won by religious enthusiasm.'

The virtues Henty extolled in his novels were manliness and

courage, modesty, truthfulness, earnestness and fair play. He reserves his great scorn for cowardice and is most consistent in his denunciations of the evils of drink. Many of the attitudes he encourages would meet with derision today. In *The Cornet of Horse*, for example, the hero, Rupert, is persuaded to wear a mail shirt as a protection against assassination. He agrees and then expresses the astonishing—to modern ears—sentiment: 'It is a useful thing against such a foe as this. I could not wear it in battle, for it would be an unfair advantage; but against an assassin all arms are fair.'

Henty has problems over evoking modesty since he cannot permit his heroes simply to perform: their deeds have to be recognized and all too often this is achieved by the threadbare device of a chance remark leading someone to insist upon the story and the hero then modestly saying what he has done. Ned in *Under Drake's Flag* dives into the sea and saves another boy from a shark, remarking modestly, if with a slight racist bias, that 'he saw no credit in the action, and that he was mightily glad to have had an opportunity of learning to do that which the negroes thought nothing of . . .'

Henty frequently makes the point that his heroes are not bookish although, if necessary, they will buckle down to some work. Thus Archie Forbes, the hero of *In Freedom's Cause* 'loved not books; but as it pleased his mother, and time often hung heavy on his hands, he did not mind devoting two or three hours a day to the tasks she set him.' Thus dutifulness as well as the value of work and learning are neatly combined.

Drink is a constant target for Henty though he does not expend time or sermons on it; in few books, however, are its evil effects not at least mentioned. In *One of the 28th* Ralph's mother gives him some parting advice before he sets off to join his regiment: 'Above all, set your face against what is the curse of our times: over-indulgence in wine. It is the ruin of thousands. Do not think it is manly to be vicious because you see others are.'

Occasionally Henty takes a different line on drink. In *The Bravest of the Brave* he depicts a splendid priest—both a fierce partisan and a man of humanity and humour—who also possesses a supply of excellent wine; and Jack, the hero, enjoys his wine. But this is unusual.

Henty liked to establish at the beginning of a story the fact that his hero is possessed of the right virtues. In *Held Fast for England* the hero, Bob Repton, is described by his schoolmaster: 'In all my experience I have never before come across a boy who had such an aptitude for getting into trouble; but I have nothing else to say against him. He is straightforward and manly. I have never known him to tell a lie to screen himself.' Bob with three other boys prevent a robbery in the house of an admiral and when the latter talks to the four boys later he delivers a homily against lying in which he says: 'Cowardice is at the bottom of half the lying in the world.'

Henty's strictures against drink are sometimes unintentionally funny. When Godfrey, the hero of *Condemned as a Nihilist*, escapes through Siberia he sends his Russian companion, Luka, into a village to buy supplies; on his return Luka informs Godfrey that he has also bought two bottles of vodka:

'That is bad, Luka.'
   'The two only cost a rouble,' Luka said calmly; 'they may be very useful to us . . .'

Considering they are about to winter alone in the forests of Siberia one ought to commend Luka's forethought. Finally, they reach Norway and while Godfrey is being fêted by a merchant, Luka is entertained by the fishermen—and gets drunk.

Godfrey was annoyed when he heard it; 'but,' as his host said, 'after being eighteen months, and, for aught I know, eighteen months before that, without touching liquor, very little would be likely to produce an effect upon him. I daresay it is his talking as much as the spirit that has turned his head; besides, you know, the lower class of Russians and Tartars are all fond of spirits.'

This somewhat mollifies Godfrey but his views are strict: 'I shall not be angry with him in the morning, because I do think that it is pardonable; but I shall talk seriously to him about it, and tell him that if he is coming home to England with me he must give up spirits. He has done without them so long that it can't be any hardship.'

Lying, Henty condemns in the strongest terms, but can none the less be positively Jesuitical when, for example, his hero is in a dangerous position among the enemy and can only, in fact, lie his way out:

'It is a nice question,' Philip said; 'but seeing that the Catholics

never keep their oaths and their promises to what they call
heretics, I think that one would be justified, not in telling a lie,
for nothing can justify that, but in availing one's self of a loophole
such as one would scorn to use to others.'

So speaks the Huguenot hero of *St. Bartholomew's Eve.*

Cyril, the hero of *When London Burned* ('A Story of Restoration
Times and the Great Fire'), is the archetypal do-gooder and
Henty's best creation in this line. He modestly never tells anyone
about any of his deeds and ends up as a model landlord when he
wins back his father's estates (sold in the King's cause). He goes to
work for a Captain Dave at the beginning of the story; the captain
asks whether he smokes: 'No, Captain Dave, I have never so much
as thought of such a thing. In France it is the fashion to take snuff,
but the habit seemed to me a useless one, and I don't think that I
should ever have taken to it.' Cyril interferes when he finds Nellie,
Captain Dave's daughter, is carrying on with an unknown cavalier;
and he does other good deeds so that Henty, having fun at the
expense of his goody-goody creation, has one character say of him:
'He is always doing good to somebody . . .'

Through Russian Snows ('Napoleon's Retreat from Moscow') is
one of Henty's two brother stories: the elder is pleasant but weak,
the younger strong and forceful. Julian, the elder, is fond of billiards
and by nineteen had given up the idea of the army. After some
trouble, however, young Frank persuades Julian to give up billiards:
'They exchanged a silent grip of the hand on the promise, and
Julian, looking more serious than usual, put on his hat and went
out.' Frank then muses: 'I can't understand myself why a fellow
finds it more difficult to say no than to say yes. If it is right to do a
thing one does it, if it is not right one leaves it alone, and the worst
one has to stand, if you don't do what other fellows want, is a certain
amount of chaff, and that hurts no one.'

The brothers go their separate ways and both are in the retreat
from Moscow, Julian serving with Ney in the French rearguard,
Frank with the British attached to the Russians. Julian saves a
little girl who turns out to be the daughter of an immensely wealthy
Russian noble; he is showered with presents and fine clothes. The
brothers then meet in St. Petersburg. Frank inspects his brother's
gifts including his vast wardrobe and then makes one of the occa-
sional unintentionally funny Henty remarks: 'That Russian count

of yours, Julian, must be a little cracked, I should think. Why, my dear boy, if you were to get stout what in the world would you do with all these things?'

Edgar, the hero of *At Aboukir and Acre* ('A Story of Napoleon's Invasion of Egypt'), has learnt boxing while at school in England. He returns to his father in Alexandria:

'Not grown quarrelsome, I hope, on the strength of your fighting, Edgar?'

'No, sir, I hope not. I never had a fight at school except the one I had three months after I got there, and I only had that one row you speak of with a clerk. I don't think it would be fair, you see, to get into rows with fellows who have no idea how thoroughly I have been taught.'

His father nodded.

'Quite right, Edgar. My ideas are that a man who can box well is much less likely to get into quarrels than one who cannot . . .'

Later, Edgar's Arab friend, Sidi, is taken prisoner by the French and Edgar resorts to a ruse to save him. He ponders upon lying: 'I am afraid that I shall have to lie. I hate that, and I would not do it for myself, but the lie will hurt no one and may save Sidi. Anyhow I won't tell more than I can help.'

Hector, on Turenne's staff in *Won by the Sword*, is a physical culture crank: 'I always had a swim in the Seine every morning when it was not closed by ice. I was told that there was nothing braced one up and made one so hardy as that; and I certainly found that even in the coldest weather I never felt the need for a cloak.' His French friends, quite rightly, want nothing to do with such barbaric practices.

Heroes are given instructions or precepts by fathers, uncles, mothers or friends of the family at the beginning of Henty stories and in no case do they later give way to temptation, even for a little while, and then redeem themselves. They possess too much moral fibre for such backslidings. Yorke, the hero of *With Roberts to Pretoria*, has a talk with his father before departing for South Africa. He vows he will be straight, put his hand to anything (in the colonies it did not matter) and avoid liquor unless ill or in extraordinary circumstances. It is agreed that after a long journey in pouring rain a little alcohol may do good, yet as Yorke's father reminds him: 'But Mr. Allnutt said that even then it was more effective if you stripped, poured some of it into your hand, and thoroughly rubbed yourself with it.'

Although Henty produced his stereotyped heroes with machine-like regularity his most interesting characters are those he permits to deviate from the norm. Henty did have a fair sense of humour although too often it is not apparent as his heroes progress rapidly from adventure to adventure.

In *Out on the Pampas*, however, he makes a contrast between the two Hardy brothers: while Charley is 'essentially of a practical disposition', Hubert 'was a far more imaginative boy . . . a new butterfly, an uncommon insect, would be irresistible to him'. This interest in birds on the part of Hubert produces one of the best passages in the whole story. The Indians attack the estate and after they have been beaten off everyone gathers and each in turn tells what happened. When it comes to Hubert to say how the Indians almost killed him he starts by describing at length how he had been in pursuit of a new duck, with special feathers. Waxing enthusiastic he ends: 'He was new, sure enough—two blue feathers under the eye.' But Charley, the practical one, cannot stand this any longer:

'Bother the duck, Hubert,' Charley put in. 'We don't care for blue feathers; we want to hear about the Indians.'

'Well, I am coming to the Indians,' Hubert said, 'but it was a new duck for all that; and if you like it, I will show it you. There!' And he took it out of his pocket and laid it on the table. No one appeared to have the slightest interest in it, or to pay any attention to it. So Hubert went on . . .

Not often does Henty indulge in such whimsy. Usually his humour is somewhat heavier handed. In *The Cornet of Horse* he has a crack at himself when he says, 'For in those days news travelled slowly, newspapers were scarcely in existence, special correspondents were a race of men undreamed of.'

Though careful never to make his heroes look foolish, Henty does occasionally poke fun at them but in such a way that his young readers might miss the point although their fathers would see it. In *One of the 28th* he has Ralph, the hero, as a junior officer with his men out in the middle of the Irish bogs searching for illicit stills. They get lost in the mist and Ralph's men are strung out in a line fifty yards apart from one another, each calling out to guide the next man: 'The shouting as the long line proceeded was prodigious, and must have astonished any stray animals that might have been grazing among the hills.' In fact Henty has described a classic junior officer's mess-up. In *St. Bartholomew's Eve* Philip's father writes to his son in France: 'I am right glad to think that a Fletcher is again cracking the skulls of Frenchmen—I mean, of course, of Catholic Frenchmen—for I regard the Huguenots, being of our religion, as half English.' It is all rather ponderous.

When Bullen, the priggish hero of *Through Three Campaigns* is in the Gold Coast with his lazy fat companion, Hallett, he constantly makes fun of the latter: joshing was the word. At the end perhaps even Henty had become bored with his hero for, when Bullen takes Hallett to task for pretending always to be bored, Hallett replies: 'My dear Bullen, you may argue forever, but if you think that you can transform me into a bustling, hustling fellow like yourself, I can tell you that you are mistaken.'

Finally, in *By Conduct and Courage* ('A Story of the Days of Nelson') there is a curious example of what might be described as Victorian sick humour. Will, the hero, rescues from drowning a girl of about fourteen (clearly destined to be his wife) although her governess has been drowned: 'You must remember that it might have been worse; you certainly cannot require a governess many more years, and will find others on whom to bestow your affection.'

Henty once said on the subject of love interest in his stories that he made a boy of twelve kiss a girl but then received an irate protest from a clergyman so cut out such passages thereafter. Again and again, he makes the point that his heroes—aged sixteen or seventeen —are uninterested in girls and should not think of marriage until much later. Only sometimes does he break this pattern. Although it is easy to mock Henty's manly heroes' lack of interest in girls, he is in fact straightforward in his treatment of a topic which was almost universally regarded as not suitable for a boy's book. Sometimes he is funny about it and often he will contrast his hero with a French or Italian boy and portray the latter, with his foreign ways, as behaving quite differently towards the opposite sex. A typical example appears in one of his earliest novels, *The Young Franc-Tireurs*:

'What pretty girls those were!'
Louis was nearly seventeen, and at seventeen a French lad considers himself a competent judge as to the appearance and manners of young ladies.

'Were they?' Percy said carelessly, with the indifference of an English boy of his age to girls. 'I did not notice it. I don't care for girls; they are always thinking about their dress, and one is afraid of touching them, in case you should spoil something. There is nothing jolly about them.'

Later in the story he makes another contrast between French manners and English manliness: 'While Louis Duburg replied seriously that he hoped that the franc-tireurs of Dijon would always do their best to deserve the kind thoughts of mademoiselles, at which piece of politeness Percy muttered "bosh".'

This attitude to girls is quite different from that portrayed briefly in *Jack Archer*, another early novel. Jack falls in love with Olga, the youngest daughter of a Russian count:

> Jack could not help glancing at Olga, for, with a midshipman's usual inflammatory tendency, he was convinced that he was hopelessly in love with the damsel. Olga coloured, and then turned away . . .

Most rare for a Henty story, in *In Freedom's Cause* where admittedly (as a device to link the activities of Wallace and Bruce) the hero continues active in the book until he is middle-aged, Archie Forbes falls in love two-thirds of the way through, wins his maid, marries her and by the end has three children. She helps him defend their castle with great courage and daring. The wooing is straight stuff:

> 'Marjory,' Archie said, when he and the girl were alone, 'I fear that you will think my wooing rude and hasty, but the times must excuse it. I would fain have waited that you might have seen more of me before I tried my fate; but in these troubled days who can say where I may be a week hence, or when I can see you again were I once separated from you! Therefore, dear, I speak at once. I love you, Marjory, and since the day when you came like an angel into my cell at Dunstaffnage I have known that I loved you, and should I never see you again could love none other. Will you wed me, love?'

She will.

A number of commentators upon Henty and his writing have suggested that he leaves the love interest out of his boys' books.

This is not the case, although the conventions within which he worked may have changed greatly. In *The Young Carthaginian*, for example, there is a pretty little love scene between the hero, Malchus, and a Gaulish maiden, Clotilde:

> 'Is she?' Malchus said carelessly. 'Were she fifty times more beautiful it would make no difference to me, for, as you know as well as I do, I love someone else.'
>
> Clotilde flushed to the brow. 'You have never said so,' she said softly.

Clotilde goes on to say that she is unworthy of Malchus and could not face the great ladies of Carthage if she were to return there with him, although at the time of the conversation they are both Roman slaves. Then they hear someone approaching: 'Malchus pressed Clotilde for a moment against his breast, and then he was alone.'

At the end of *Orange and Green*, Walter marries his Claire, who had nursed him when wounded. Walter's mother is surprised to learn he is serious:

> 'You don't mean to say, Walter, that you have been falling in love at your age?'
>
> 'You forget, dear,' Captain Davenant said, coming to Walter's rescue, 'that Walter is no longer a boy. Three years of campaigning . . .'
>
> 'And is there anything in what your father says?' Mrs Davenant asked . . .
>
> 'Yes, mother,' he answered manfully. 'I am engaged to Claire Conyers . . .'

In *For the Temple*, when the hero is off to fight, his girl friend Mary says: 'I thought you would decide so, John; and much as I love you—for I do love you, John—I would rather part with you so, never to see you again, than that you should draw back now.'

Henty is not prepared to allow these love scenes to get out of hand. Francis, the hero of *The Lion of St. Mark*, is teased by his Venetian friend, Matteo, who suggests how fortunate he is in having rescued the two heiresses of a leading merchant:

> 'Nonsense!' Francis said, colouring. 'How can you talk so absurdly, Matteo? I am only a boy, and it will be years before I can think of marriage . . .'

A friend of Giulia, the heiress Francis is destined to marry, asks:

'And does Francis never pay you compliments, Giulia?'
'Never!' Giulia said decidedly. 'It would be hateful of him if he did.'

. . . .

'From which I gather,' Giustiniani said smiling, 'that this English lad's bluntness of speech pleases you more than it does Maria?'

'It pleases Maria too,' Giulia said, 'though she may choose to say that it doesn't. And I don't think it quite right to discuss him at all when we all owe him as much as we do.'

Giustiniani glanced at Maria and gave a little significant nod. 'I do not think Giulia regards Francisco in quite the brotherly way that you do, Maria,' he whispered presently to her.

When at the end of the story Francis asks the merchant, Polani, for his daughter's hand and the merchant consents, the reader may be forgiven—for there have been a good many hints by these vivacious Venetian girls—that the hero will now go to his love and at least embrace her. Instead, Henty plays a trick, for the next paragraph begins: 'Two months later the marriage of Francis Hammond and Giulia Polani took place . . .'

Often, however, there is no love interest of even the mildest kind anywhere in the book, although at the end in his tidying-up operation Henty usually marries his hero to someone. Thus Horace, the hero of *In Greek Waters*, saves a girl and her mother in the middle of the story; at the very end he meets them again at a party and we are simply told that in due course he made the girl his wife.

In *Under Wellington's Command* (the sequel to *With Moore at Corunna*—the only occasion when Henty had the same hero in two books) Terence saves a cousin, Mary, and while he is in the Peninsular she is back in Ireland using her fortune to help his father rebuild the family house. She means to have Terence. He writes long letters home full of boring military detail; Mary writes back—not interested in the military detail but 'now, on the other hand, I should like to know all about this young woman who helped you to get out of prison.'

In *A Roving Commission* ('Through the Black Insurrection of Hayti') the hero rescues the daughter of a French planter from a savage dog. Myra is appointed to show Nat round the estate:

'Mamma said I might act as your guide, and show you about the plantation, and the slave houses, and everywhere. I have never had a boy friend, and I should think it was very nice.'

'My dear,' her mother said with a smile, 'it is not altogether discreet for a young lady to talk in that way.'

Needless to say Nat marries Myra at the end and there is a tender little love scene when he proposes to her on the verandah.

The Treasure of the Incas is one of Henty's straight adventure stories—not a history—and the motivation for the two brothers departing for South America is love. The elder has been turned down by his prospective father-in-law on the grounds that he is penniless and so sets off with his younger brother Bertie to Peru to look for treasure which, needless to say, he finds. As Bertie says to his elder infatuated brother: 'Well, of course I cannot understand it, Harry, and it seems to me that one girl is very like another; she may be a bit prettier than the average, but I suppose that comes to all the same thing in another twenty years. I can understand a man getting awfully fond of his ship, especially when she is a clipper.'

Possibly the funniest Henty comment upon the subject of love appears in the long short story, 'In the Hands of the Malays'. The hero saves the girl he is to marry from the traditional fate 'worse than death' at the hands of a pirate chief. The girl shudders: 'From what fate have you saved me! But it would not have been so, for I would have killed myself.' To this her Dutch husband-to-be answers, prosaically, that the pirate might not have given her the opportunity to do so. Romance in their case is clearly destined for routine practicality.

CHAPTER FIVE

Attitudes: Stereotypes—Race—Empire

IN HIS PREFACE to *St. George for England* which was published in 1885, the year of the Berlin Conference which signalled the European Scramble for Africa, Henty wrote: 'The courage of our forefathers has created the greatest empire in the world around a small and in itself insignificant island; if this empire is ever lost, it will be by the cowardice of their descendants.' In an article entitled 'A Great Imperialist', the Rev. Hugh Pruen* says. 'Above all, Henty is the great Imperialist. His writing days coincided with the high-water mark of Jingoism, with the premierships of Disraeli, Salisbury and Rosebery, and with the Jubilees, when the English were conscious for a brief period of a manifest destiny to which Kipling was to give matchless expression in his "Recessional".'

It has become fashionable, with hindsight, for writers about this period to detect growing doubts, while historians regard the Boer War as a turning point that caused a questioning of the imperial idea from which it was never quite to recover, yet if others had doubts Henty appeared to have none. Writing for the *Boys' Own Paper* just before his death—the article was published posthumously in December 1902—Henty said:

> To endeavour to inculcate patriotism in my books has been one of my main objects, and so far as it is possible to know, I have not been unsuccessful in that respect. I know that very many boys have joined the cadets and afterwards gone into the Army through reading my stories, and at many of the meetings at which I have spoken officers of the Army and Volunteers have assured me that my books have been effectual in bringing young fellows into the Army—not so much into the rank and file as among the officers.

Henty was not an inspired writer; he was remarkably consistent in

* *The Henty Society Bulletin*, Number 5, September 1978.

the values which he extolled in book after book. His attitudes are often curiously mixed and though he may be termed a High Tory as far as patriotism and empire are concerned there is also a broad liberalism to be discerned in his approach to aspects of education, religion or, sometimes, other races.

In one of his short stories, 'A Brush with the Chinese', Henty produces some of his most unpleasant stereotypes and racialism is strident. War has been declared with China, 'in consequence of her continued evasions of the treaty she had made with us', and a naval ship goes to deal with some Chinese junks. 'The valour of the Chinese evaporated as they saw the boats approaching, and scores of them leapt overboard and swam for shore.' The two midshipmen heroes take a punitive party into a village; the first lieutenant's instructions to the senior midshipman are:

'Mr. Fothergill, take your party into the village and set fire to the houses; shoot down every man you see. This place is a nest of pirates. I will capture that battery and then join you.'

Fothergill and his sailors at once entered the village. The men had already fled; the women were turned out of the houses, and these were immediately set on fire. The tars regarded the whole affair as a glorious joke, and raced from house to house, making a hasty search in each for concealed valuables before setting it on fire.

There is, however, a turn of fortune and the two midshipmen are captured. They imagine their captors will take them to Canton to claim a reward: 'I expect they are discussing it now; do you hear what a jabber they are kicking up?' They realize that the Chinese hope to make a profit out of their capture: 'As to the idea that mercy has anything to do with it, we may as well put it out of our minds. The Chinaman, at the best of times, has no feeling of pity in his nature, and after their defeat it is certain they would have killed us at once had they not hoped to do better by us.' These strictures come oddly from those who had not for a moment questioned the lieutenant's instructions to kill every man in the village.

The Chinese build a bamboo cage in which they carry the wretched, cramped prisoners from village to village and put them on display. Jack, the elder, says: 'I don't care for the pain, Percy, so much as the humiliation of the thing. To be stared at and poked at as if we were wild beasts by these curs, when with half a dozen of our men we could send a hundred of them scampering, I feel as if I could choke with rage.' It is a beastly little story; the worst element is the automatic acceptance of the fact that it is right for the British to be brutal for they, after all, are simply punishing the Chinese for breaking a treaty obligation.

It is important, and difficult, to obtain a balance. Henty, with many of his countrymen, believed in the superiority of the British, the rightness of Empire, the vital contribution to world order made by the Pax Britannica. A generation later, in 1919, thousands of Englishmen leapt to the defence of General Dyer after the brutal massacre at Amritsar which did so much to change the political climate in British India; many of those Englishmen would have been nurtured on Henty's attitudes. In a famous appraisal of the British Empire the American philosopher, George Santayana, said: 'Never since the heroic days of Greece has the world had such a sweet, just, boyish master,' and Henty would surely have agreed with that encomium for it fitted the stereotype of his manly hero who, whatever the time and place of the story, was, in fact, a prototype District Officer. In 1933 Freya Stark wrote: 'We spend our time creating a magnificent average type of Englishman, the finest instrument in the world . . .' This, pre-eminently, was what Henty wanted to do, and the aim of all his writing for boys was to teach the values of the kind which would produce one of Santayana's 'just, boyish masters'.

Henty also believed in money-making and the diligence with which he ensures that almost all his heroes end up moderately if not outright rich in part, perhaps, reflects his own life for, despite his voluminous output, he was never a wealthy man. In *Out on the Pampas* Hubert, the younger, whimsical Hardy brother, expresses his satisfaction to his father, after they shoot an ostrich, that the others have escaped: 'Yes, Hubert, but the feathers are really worth money.' This kind of mercenary sentiment appears again and again.

Henty was opposed to radicalism in all its forms. The father of the two boys in *The Young Franc-Tireurs* tell them: 'Radical opinions may be very wise and very excellent for a nation, for aught I know, but it is certain that they are fatal to the discipline of an army. My own opinion, as you know, is that they are equally fatal for a country, but that is a matter of opinion only; but of the fact

that a good Radical makes an extremely bad soldier I am quite
clear . . .'

In *Jack Archer* Henty made a point that coloured a great deal of
his historical writing: 'Few nations have done more fighting than
we, and, roughly speaking, the wars have always been popular.'
Later in the same story Jack and a friend heroically save sixteen
sailors during a storm. Jack's worldly friend remarks afterwards:
'However, old boy, we did a good night's work. We saved sixteen
lives, we got no end of credit, and the chief says he shall send a
report in to the Admiral; so we shall be mentioned in despatches,
and it will help us for promotion when we have passed.' There is
nothing like an eye to the main chance and, though Henty constantly
tries to inculcate the values of manliness and leadership necessary
to produce leaders for the Empire, he seems equally concerned with
rising: making a fortune, being promoted, achieving success and
recognition—and sometimes titles as well.

Essentially Victorian thoughts and judgements imbue all Henty's
books. Early in *The Young Carthaginian*, for example, the father of
Malchus, the hero, instructs his son:

> 'I fear not,' Hamilcar said gravely shaking his head. 'It seems to
> be the fate of all nations, that as they grow in wealth so they lose
> their manly virtues. With wealth comes corruption, indolence,
> a reluctance to make sacrifices, and a weakening of the feeling of
> patriotism. Power falls into the hands of the ignorant many.'

A disdain for the democratic process of 'one man one vote' is
certainly apparent in a number of the books and was, at least in part,
influenced by what Henty had seen in Paris at the time of the
Commune. Hamilcar, still instructing his son, says: 'I should not,
of course, propose giving to them a vote; to bestow the suffrage
upon the ignorant, who would simply follow the demagogues who
would use them as tools, would be the height of madness.' And he
draws a parallel with Tyre; 'This triumph of the democracy in
Tyre, as might be expected, proved the ruin of that city.' Curiously,
Henty never appears to see any irony in all these judgements in the
context of a possible application to Britain and her Empire.

In a very different story, *A Final Reckoning* ('A Tale of Bush Life
in Australia'), Henty has a good Tory squire write to a friend in
London in order to find a new village schoolmaster:

'I don't want a chap who will cram all sorts of new notions into the heads of the children,' the squire said; 'I don't think it would do them any good, or fit them any better for their stations. The boys have got to be farm labourers and the girls to be their wives, and if they can read really well and write fairly it's about as much as they want in the way of learning . . .'

Thriftiness was a prime Victorian virtue and in *For the Temple* there is a typically nineteenth-century comment on the poor: 'There were poor in Palestine, for there will be poor everywhere so long as human nature remains as it is, and some men are idle and self-indulgent while others are industrious and thrifty . . .' Indeed Henty stories are studded with pieces of homely Victorian philosophy, often emanating from unlikely sources. Thus the mother of Amuba, the hero of *The Cat of Bubastes*, is queen of the Rebu people; when it is clear they will be conquered by the Egyptians she commits suicide. Before doing so, however, she has a last message for her son: 'There is no greater happiness on a throne than in a cottage. Men make their own happiness, and a man may be respected even though only a slave.' This particular story, indeed, is studded with Victorian precepts such as 'honest men need never fear an encounter with rogues'.

Sometimes, if his story is set well in the past, Henty feels obliged to remind his readers that he is really writing about manly English boys of his own time. In the preface to *The Lion of St. Mark*, set in fourteenth-century Venice, he says:

'The historical portion of the story is drawn from Hazlitt's *History of the Republic of Venice*, and with it I have woven the adventures of an English boy endowed with a full share of that energy and pluck which, more than any other qualities, have made the British empire the greatest the world has ever seen.'

The hero, Francis, later moralizes to his friend Matteo: 'That is all very well, Matteo; but to do anything great you have got to do small things first.'

Much of Henty's moralizing must appear tedious to a modern reader; sometimes, because of its unexpected form, perhaps it is refreshing. Unusually in the preface to *One of the 28th* ('A Tale of Waterloo'), Henty claims that the real hero of the story is a woman and, defending women's courage, he says: 'Indeed, my own somewhat extensive experience leads me to go even farther, and to assert that among a civil population, untrained to arms, the average woman is cooler and more courageous than the average man. Women are nervous about little matters; they may be frightened at a mouse or at a spider; but in the presence of real danger, when shells are bursting in the streets, and rifle bullets flying thickly, I have seen them standing knitting at their doors and talking to their friends across the street when not a single man was to be seen.'

Henty regarded public schools and the rough and tumble of boarding school life as vital instruments in producing young men of the sort he believed the country required to be its leaders; and boys would be rounded off into good fellows by having the stuffing knocked out of them. Again in *One of the 28th*, the hero, Ralph, has joined his regiment with another young chap, Stapleton, who is being given a rough time because he has not been to school and does not take easily to practical jokes. Ralph patronizes him:

'Well I do think your four months with the regiment have done you a world of good, Stapleton. You certainly were a stuck-up sort of personage when you came on board in the Thames. I think it is an awful mistake for a fellow to be educated at home, instead of being sent to school; they are sure to have to suffer for it afterwards.'

'Well, I have suffered for it to some extent,' Stapleton said. 'The lessons I got at first were sharp ones; but they certainly did me good.'

'There is no doubt about that,' Ralph agreed; 'and I think there is a good deal of credit due to you, Stapleton, for having taken things in the right way.'

Stapleton, of course, by admitting his error and the beneficial effect of the 'lessons', and by allowing Ralph to lecture him, is well on the way to qualifying as a first-class fellow himself.

The subject of rewards comes up at the end of *By Pike and Dyke* when the hero, Ned, is in the service of the notoriously parsimonious Queen Elizabeth. His father lectures him: 'Fair words butter no parsnip, Ned. Honour and royal service empty the purse instead of filling it. It behoves you to think these matters over.' Ned, however, goes on to be knighted and for once Elizabeth sees he also has money. The relevant chapter bears the heading: 'Pay as well as honour.'

There are further useful precepts in *Held Fast for England*. Bob, the hero, is lectured by a clerk in his uncle's counting house: 'There is nothing more unfortunate for a young man belonging to the middle classes than to have no fixed occupation.' Later Bob's uncle says to him: 'The happiest man, in my opinion, is he who has something to do, and yet not too much; who can, by being free from anxieties regarding it, view his business as an occupation and a pleasure, and who is its master and not its slave.'

On the way out to Gibraltar, Bob goes ashore at a Portuguese port and is tempted to assist some English sailors in a fight with the authorities. On his return to the ship he tells the captain, who gives an interesting reply:

'It is lucky that you kept clear of the row. It is all nonsense talking about countrymen; it wasn't an affair of nationality at all. Nobody would think of interfering if he saw a party of drunken sailors in an English port fighting with the constables. If he did interfere, it ought to be on the side of the law. Why, then, should anyone take the part of drunken sailors in a foreign port against the guardians of the peace? To do so is an act of the grossest folly. In the first place, the chances are in favour of getting your head laid open with a sword-cut. These fellows know they don't stand a chance against Englishmen's fists . . .'

The advice is sage; the ending typical, partly for the caution, partly for the bombast. Indeed, there is often a realistic caution about Henty: his heroes may perform impossible deeds but he makes them hold back at the foolhardy, and sometimes produces homilies in the text about taking risks unnecessarily. Even so, he could never resist pitting English fists against foreigners'.

Henty certainly believed in the efficacy of flogging, both for boys as punishment for honourable offences—there are frequent references to his heroes having been flogged at school—and for criminals. When Godfrey, the hero of *Condemned as a Nihilist*, is in his Siberian prison he is asked by a Russian whether English peasants are not beaten by their masters:

'Beaten! I should think not,' Godfrey said. 'Nobody is beaten with us, though I think it would be a capital thing if, instead of shutting up people in prison for small crimes, they had a good flogging. It would do them a deal more good, and it would be better for their wives and families, who have to get on as best they can while they are shut up.'

Indeed, *Condemned as a Nihilist* is crammed with splendid Henty political strictures upon radicalism, women in politics and atheism. Godfrey has a conversation with a Russian who tells him of the Nihilists:

'They have driven the Czar to war against them; they have strengthened the hands of the men who will use their acts as an excuse for the extremest measures of repression; they have ranged on the other side all the moderate men like myself, who, desirous of constitutional changes, shrink with horror from a revolution heralded by deeds of bloodshed and murder.'

'I quite agree with you,' Godfrey said warmly. 'Men must be mad who could counsel such abominable plans.'

Later he is told:

'One of the most extraordinary things connected with the movement is that women play a large part in it. Being in the thick of every conspiracy they are the life and soul of the movement, and they are of all classes. There are a score of women for whose arrest the authorities would pay any money, and yet they elude every effort. It is horrible. This is what comes of women going to Switzerland and learning to look upon religion as a myth and all authority as hateful, and to have wild dreams of an impossible state of affairs such as never has existed in this world. It is horrible, but it is pitiable. The prisons of the land are full of victims; trains of prisoners set off monthly for Siberia . . .'

Henty, one feels, would not have looked kindly upon the suffragettes during the decade after his death. And Godfrey has his own comment upon those sent to Siberia: 'I cannot understand what the motive of government can be in sending thousands of such wretches out here instead of hanging them.'

There are interesting twists to Henty; he was not, for instance, a total philistine. The doctor in *In Greek Waters* lectures Horace, the hero, on the beauties of Turkish architecture (they have been taken prisoner); and speaks of Constantinople:

'Why, man, we may be a great nation, intelligent and civilized, and all that; but when it comes to an appreciation of the beautiful we are poor bodies, indeed, by the side of the Turk, whom we in our mightiness are accustomed to consider a barbarian. I know what you are going to say,' he went on, as Horace was going to speak. 'There is tyranny and oppression, and evil rule, and corruption, and other bad things in that beautiful city. I grant you all that, but that has nothing to do with my argument. He may be a heathen, he may be ignorant, he may be what we call uncivilized; but the Turk has a grand soul or he never would have imagined a dream of beauty like this.'

The doctor is a refreshing figure among Henty's stern empire-builders.

Henty heroes are all gentlemen and incipient members of the establishment, a term Henty would have relished. In *A Jacobite Exile*, the hero's father cautions him at the beginning of the tale about supporting lost causes: 'I believe in fighting where there is some chance, even a slight one, of success, but I regard it as an act of folly to throw away a life when no good can come of it.' There is a possibility that William III will be assassinated, and the father says: 'The Dutchman must see that English gentlemen, however ready to fight against him fairly, would have no hand in so dastardly a plot as this.' Henty heroes always come out on the winning side: they may start as romantic Jacobites; they end up making their peace with the king and so retaining—or recovering—their estates. It is all part of Henty's support for the established order.

Henty's morality about gentlemen is expressed simply in *A March on London* when the hero's father tells Edgar: 'If, my boy, you should some day go to court and mingle in public affairs, above all things keep yourself clear of any party . . . The duty of an English gentleman is simple: he must work for his country, regardless altogether of personal interest.' Later, returning to a familiar Henty theme, the father also says: 'Unhappily, my son, the masses do not think. They believe what it pleases them to believe, and what the men who go about stirring up sedition tell them.' But the high sentiments about country and no party are somewhat spoilt further on when Edgar—very much in the ascendant—returns home, allowing his father to say, '[You] have placed your foot so firmly on the ladder, that 'tis your own fault if you do not rise high.'

There are two boys, friends, in *A March on London* and one of their many deeds is to rescue a rich Fleming merchant from the

London mob; at the end he bestows a large estate on each of them. Albert, the son of a knight, asks his father whether he should accept:

'There can be no mistake in the deed, father; but can I accept such a gift at the hands of the Fleming?'
'That you can, my son, and without any hesitation. Van Voorden is known to be the richest Fleming in England.'

Albert marries Ursula and of his son's marriage Sir Ralph says: 'She is a fair maid, and her father is a right good fellow, though but a city knight. Still, others of higher rank than yourself have married in the city, and as Sir Robert has no other children, and is said to be one of the wealthiest of the London citizens, she will doubtless come to you better endowed than will Aline [to Edgar]'. Snobbery, place, money, position—these are the Victorian preoccupations at the height of Empire. The chapter is called 'Well Settled' and we are told: 'Neither of the two young knights ever rode to the wars again . . .' One often feels that Henty is more in favour of his heroes being well settled than of all their preceding adventures.

Radicalism, as has already been noted, upset Henty. In *No Surrender!* ('A Tale of the Rising of La Vendée') he makes one character say: 'There were two writers, Voltaire and Rousseau, who have done enormous mischief. Both of them perceived that the state of things was wrong, but they went to extremes, made fun of the church, and attacked institutions of all sorts.' In *Out With Garibaldi* Henty obviously favours Cavour and Garibaldi—the one for being moderate, the other for being romantic—but cannot tolerate the radical Republican Mazzini.

In one of his last books (published posthumously) *With the Allies to Pekin* there is, despite the general assumption of imperial-British right to interfere in China, also a touch of Henty the former war correspondent. The father explains to his son, 'And yet, Rex, a good deal of allowance must be made for them.' Condescending, but he goes on to make a number of points: that the Chinese dislike foreigners; that the British had imposed themselves upon the Chinese because the latter refused to sell opium; that the foreigners had forced them to open their ports to trade; that they had invaded them with a vast crowd of missionaries and, worse still, that the missionaries had taken converts under their protection and set themselves up as local powers. This enlightened man concludes:

'All these things are odious to the mass of the people, and when, as at present, they find the whole of the European powers engaged in a general grab of fresh ports, they say this thing must stop.' Later he adds: 'To my mind, the game of grab that has been going on of late has been shocking.'

Momentarily chastened by these reflections from his father, young Rex Bateman says: 'Well, I don't think that I ever thought of it in that light, Father, but it certainly does seem rough on them that we should seize port after port on the smallest pretext, and send our people interfering with their customs and religions all over the country.' This mood does not last; later young Bateman can say: 'They have attacked us and perpetrated the most horrible massacres all over the country; they have lied through thick and thin; they are treacherous and cruel brutes, who will certainly show no mercy if they capture the place, so that I shall feel that I am fighting in a good cause, and that these men deserve all they will get.' And one of the girls Rex has rescued earlier says: 'I wish I were a boy. I should like to help kill some of the Boxers.'

Finally, in this book, there occurs a remarkable passage of amorality. The victorious allied armies have been looting and Mr. Bateman instructs his son in what to look out for and buy from the soldiers since they will not know the worth of what they have taken. Looting may be wrong but the commercial instinct takes over. Mr. Bateman supplies Rex with ample money and, as a result of his purchases, they make a handsome profit at second hand, as it were, from the looting activities of others. At the end, however, Henty is constrained to say: 'It must be admitted, however, that the conduct of the troops, especially of the Russians, Germans, and French, cannot but have greatly heightened the hatred felt by the Chinese for the "foreign devils".'

Henty is a continual purveyor of racial generalizations. Thus in *The Young Franc-Tireurs* he says: 'Perhaps in the whole world there is no class of people so completely engrossed by the thought of gain as are the French bourgeois and rustic population.' In *Jack Archer* he is more complimentary. When a fire has to be extinguished and the French do the work, Henty says: 'There was no water, no means whatever of extinguishing the flames, but the active little Frenchmen did not lose a minute.'

This historical-imperial comparison with Victorian Britain is always emphasized. In *The Young Carthaginian* Henty's sympathies are with the expanding and vigorous Rome as against the old, corrupt Carthage, and underlying that sympathy is an implied comparison between the Roman and British empires. As he says in his preface: 'Thus then, although we may feel sympathy for the failure and fate of the noble and chivalrous Hannibal himself, we cannot regret that Rome came out conqueror in the strife, and was left free to carry out her great work of civilization.'

At the end of *The Cat of Bubastes*, when Amuba returns to his homeland he first overthrows the prevailing tyranny and then becomes king. His friend, Chebron, the son of the High Priest of Egypt, is cast in the role of counsellor. Having regained his throne and driven out the Egyptians in remote Rebu land, Amuba gets down to reforms in the fashion of a Cromer:

> Once prepared for war Amuba turned his attention to the internal affairs of the country. Many of the methods of government of Egypt were introduced. Irrigation was carried out on a large scale, and the people were taught no longer to depend solely on their flocks and herds. Stone took the place of mud in the buildings of the towns, rigorous justice was enforced throughout the land, wagons and carts similar to those of Egypt took the place of pack animals, which had hitherto been used for transport; improved methods of agriculture were taught, and contentment and plenty reigned in the land.

Finally this paragon persuades the people—though here he does meet resistance—to change their religion and adopt the monotheism he has learnt from Chebron's father and Ruth, an Israelite. There is another nice imperial touch when Amuba reflects: 'He was well aware that the success of the work was to no small extent due to the earnestness with which Mysa and Ruth had laboured among the wives and daughters of the nobles.'

In *The Lion of St. Mark* there is a further instance of racial stereotyping: 'Giuseppi had plenty of shrewdness . . . possessing as he did plenty of the easy mendacity so general among the lower classes of the races inhabiting countries bordering on the Mediterranean.' Yet racist as Henty often appears, there are surprising exceptions. When Roger, the hero of *By Right of Conquest*, has to part from an Indian girl, Malinche, he reflects: 'It is as bad, as it was saying goodbye to Dorothy and Agnes. Colour does not matter much, after all. Malinche is just as good and kind as if she were white.' At the end of this same story Roger has married an Indian, admittedly a princess, and with his spoil he buys himself an estate in Devon: 'She bore Roger several children, and to this day many of the first families in Devonshire are proud that there runs in their veins the blood of the Aztec princess.'

Negroes and natives of all varieties feature often enough in Henty's books. None is more constantly stereotyped by the author than the African negro, often referred to as a 'nigger'. In *Maori and Settler*, long before the main characters reach New Zealand, the following conversation takes place:

> 'The negroes amuse me most,' Marion said. 'They seem to be always laughing. I never saw such merry people.'
> 'They are like children,' her father said. 'The slightest thing causes them amusement. It is one of the signs of a low type of intellect when people are given to laugh at trifles.'

In this instance, however, Henty provides a twist, for the girl replies, though now she is speaking of the Brazilians: 'Then the natives ought to be very intelligent, for as a whole they appeared to me to be a serious race.'

Henty seems to have had a marked antipathy towards the Jews whose appearance as casual characters in most of his books is usually in an uncomplimentary light. In *Held Fast for England* there are such throwaway remarks as 'We know that there are many Jews and others most anxious to leave the town before the enemy begin to bombard it . . .' while later the hero, Bob, who is to sail to Tangier with some Jews as fellow-passengers, reflects: 'The boatman will know that I have something to do with the governor, and the two Jews will certainly know that I don't belong to the Rock. If they find that the Moors have joined the Spaniards, these Jews may try to get through themselves by denouncing me.'

In that curious Henty potboiler, *In Greek Waters*, there are further racial generalizations. Mr. Beveridge is a rich Englishman who takes his own sloop out to aid the Greeks in their war of independence in the 1820s. He engages a naval officer, William Martyn, as captain of his ship. Martyn at one point tells his employer: 'I have great doubts whether they will ever submit to discipline. Their idea of fighting for centuries has been simply to shoot down an enemy from behind the shelter of rocks. I would as lief undertake to discipline an army of Malays, who, in a good many respects, especially in the handiness with which they use their knives, are a good deal like the Greeks.' Mr. Beveridge adds his own racial quotient to this: 'There is one broad distinction: the Malays have no past . . .' Martyn knows when to hold his peace although in his opinion 'the entire extirpation of the Greek race would be no loss to the world in general'; while another character, Tom, a fisherman who is also a member of Mr. Beveridge's motley crew, opines: 'But they ain't dependable, none of those Mediterranean chaps are, whether they are Greeks or Italians or Spaniards . . .'

Later there is a conversation between Beveridge and his sixteen-year-old son, Horace:

> 'I take it, of course, that you are as interested in the struggle as I am.'
>
> 'Well, not so interested perhaps, father. I feel, of course, that it is a horrible thing that a people like the Greeks, to whom we all owe so much, should be kept in slavery by the Turks, who have never done any good to mankind that I know of . . .'

Horace warns his father to give weapons rather than money to the insurgents since, he has heard, the upper-class Greeks are as bad (or corrupt) as the Turkish Pashas. Mr. Beveridge agrees and adds a point about the Jews: 'You see in a country that is enslaved political and other careers are closed, and the young men devote themselves to making money. You see that in the history of the Jews.'

Beric the Briton was published in 1893, halfway between the two Jubilees when so many of Victoria's subjects were brought to London to witness the splendours of the imperial capital. Beric, who fights the Romans first under Boadicea and then in Italy when he has escaped from slavery under Nero, is finally pardoned and converted to their way. He returns home to act on their behalf. Now a district commissioner, as it were, Beric assures the Iceni

> that he had been sent by the emperor Galba, who desired to see peace and contentment reign in Britain, and had therefore appointed a countryman of their own as governor of their province, and that, though he should make Norwich the place of his government, he should journey about throughout the country, listen to all complaints and grievances, and administer justice against offenders, whatever their rank and station.
>
> Above all he exhorted them to tranquillity and obedience.

'Rome wishes you well,' he said, 'and would fain see you as contented beneath her sway as is Gaul, and as are the other countries she has conquered and occupied. We form part of the Roman Empire now, that is as fixed and irrevocable as the rising and setting of the sun. To struggle against Rome is as great a folly as for an infant to wrestle with a giant. But once forming a part of the empire we shall share in its greatness. Towns will rise over the land and wealth increase, and all will benefit by the civilization that Rome will bring to us.' He addressed similar speeches to the people at each halting place . . .

There is nothing like a convert. It is a perfect parable for the spread of the British empire.

It would be pleasant to end on this note for at least such a passage contains a certain innocence. But that would not be possible as Henty's last books—those published from 1900 onwards—became strident in both their imperialism and racialism. *A Roving Commission* is possibly the most racist of all his books. The preface begins: 'Horrible as were the atrocities of which the monsters of the French Revolution were guilty, they paled before the fiendish outrages committed by their black imitators in Hayti.' At the end of the preface, after another of his semi-apologias for slavery, Henty says: 'Unless some strong white power should occupy the island and enforce law and order, sternly repress crime, and demand a certain amount of labour from all able-bodied men, there seems no hope that any amelioration can take place in the present situation.' Halfway through the story an officer says of the mulattoes:

'Poor beggars . . . they are neither one thing nor the other! . . . The negroes don't like them because of their strain of white blood. They are treated as if they are pariahs . . .'

'It is hard on them,' Glover [the hero] said, 'but one can't be surprised that the whites do fight shy of them. Great numbers of them are brutes and no mistake, ready for any crime and up to any wickedness. There is lots of good in the niggers; they are merry fellows; and I must say for these old French planters they use their slaves a great deal better than they are as a rule treated by our planters in Jamaica.'

Here we have condemnation of miscegenation; the stereotype of the merry nigger; the liberal attack not so much upon slavery as upon bad masters; and overall the acceptance of the *status quo* which is the hallmark of the the Henty hero. Blacks are referred to as niggers throughout.

The hero and his sailors rescue some slaves from a slaving post: 'They [the slaves] had now come to the conclusion that their new captors were really friends, and with the light-heartedness of their race laughed and chattered as if their past sufferings were already forgotten.' The stereotypes continue, at one point designed to show almost idyllic black-white relations—of a paternalist kind: 'In the women's huts the scene was still more interesting. The little children ran up to Nat with a new born confidence in white men. Some of the women brought up babies to show him . . .' Henty also makes his contribution to one of the most ugly imperial-racial attitudes: that blacks smell. 'The windows and doors stood open, and the evening breeze cleared the huts of the effluvium always present where a number of negroes congregate together.' Henty, who had served in the army and lived rough in mining camps, might just as well have recalled the effluvium from a barracks or mining camp dormitory.

Monsieur Duchesne, whose daughter Nat is destined to marry, tells him of the state of affairs in Hayti:

> 'We should have an assembly composed entirely of slaves, and these slaves would at once vote that all the land and property in the island should be divided among themselves. What think you of that, Monsieur Glover?'
>
> 'It would be madness indeed,' Nat agreed.

Inevitably, Duchesne goes on to say: 'But, nevertheless, the negroes are like children, they can be led by a little talk . . .' Fleeing to the hills at one point in the story, Nat says: 'I thought they would hardly come up as far as this; negroes are not given to work unless they are obliged to . . .'

Henty, despite the glaring prejudices which emerge in this particular book, does however try to paint a fair picture of the leader of the slave revolt, Toussaint L'Ouverture, although when Nat goes to see him he finds 'he was a wonderfully intelligent fellow for a negro'. Reflecting upon the likely outcome of the revolt Nat says: 'I have no doubt that if the last white man left the island, and slavery were abolished for ever, the negroes would be very much worse off than they were before, and I should think they would most likely go back to the same idle, savage sort of life that they live in Africa.' Nat parleys with Toussaint and Henty puts into his mouth a perfectly correct historical-imperial justification for Britain not giving guarantees against slavery: 'It would mean absolute ruin to our islands; for you know as well as I do that your people are not disposed for work, and would never make steady labourers if allowed to live in their own way. Then you see, were slavery abolished altogether in this island, it would be difficult in the extreme to continue it in others.'

At the end of the story, instead of the usual Henty paragraph about Nat being happily married and becoming an honoured pillar of his local neighbourhood, there is an historical footnote:

> At the end of the war, Toussaint was virtually Dictator of Hayti. He governed strongly and well, but as he was determined to admit no interference on the part of the French, he was finally treacher-ously seized by them, carried to France, and there died, it is said by starvation, in prison. His forebodings as to the unfitness of the blacks for self-government have been fulfilled to the letter. Civil wars, insurrections, and massacres have been the rule rather than the exception; the island has been gradually going down in the scale of civilization, and the majority of the blacks are as savage, ignorant and superstitious as their forefathers in Africa. Fetish worship and human sacrifices are carried on in secret, and the fairest island in the western seas lies sunk in the lowest degra-dation—a proof of the utter incapacity of the negro race to evolve, or even maintain, civilization, without the example and the curb of a white population among them.

The stereotype of blacks as lazy, childlike, without capacity, and still more the feeling of contempt for them are glaring in this novel, and Henty must take a full share of responsibility for propa-gating the kind of views which have done such damage to British relations with African or Asian people during the present century. Nor is the retrospective defence of such attitudes—that they were normal for that period in history—really tenable. To suggest that Henty was expressing no more than what half his contemporaries felt is to denigrate his powers and influence. He was a propagandist —for empire and British interests—and a highly successful one, too, in his way. He held very strong views, he wanted to get them across and achieved a high success in doing so through the medium of his boy's books. Such views were not incidental to the story; as Henty often claimed, he set out to instruct as well as amuse. His books were still to be found on school shelves fifty years after his death and at least some of the racial arrogance which, unhappily, has been so marked a characteristic of British behaviour in what is now termed 'The Third World' can be attributed to his influence.

PART THREE

The Books

CHAPTER SIX

The Henty Range

THE SPREAD OF subjects, in period and in setting, covered by Henty was enormous. Of the eighty-two titles listed in the appendix* all but four are full-length stories, while *In the Hands of the Malays, John Hawke's Fortune, In the Hands of the Cave Dwellers* and *A Soldier's Daughter* are really long short stories. They range from pre-Christian times to the opening of the twentieth century and the Boer War. They are mainly, though not exclusively, concerned with military history; sometimes with naval actions; and sometimes, though rarely, with social and political developments. Certain subjects, for instance the handling of boats or mining, are dealt with expertly, reflecting Henty's own experience. The nineteenth-century wars are often treated journalistically by Henty the war correspondent rather than historically—and this is especially the case with a dozen stories written about events which took place during the last quarter of the nineteenth century.

Henty wrote four of his better historical novels about the ancient world and to his chagrin found that the sales of three of them were amongst his lowest because their heroes were not English lads. The first in time, *The Cat of Bubastes*, deals with ancient Egypt; the second, *The Young Carthaginian*, with the story of Hannibal's invasion of Italy. We then move to the first century in which *Beric the Briton* and *For the Temple* are set: the former concerns Boadicea and Nero's Rome, the latter is the story of the destruction of the temple at Jerusalem and the diaspora of the Jews under Titus.

Henty then skips the Dark Ages, placing his next story in the eighth century at the time of King Alfred; this, *The Dragon and the Raven*, though good in parts, is not one of his more distinguished books as far as the history is concerned, whereas the next book in time, *Wulf the Saxon*, which covers the Norman Conquest, is historically one of his best.

* See p. 181.

Winning His Spurs (one of the poorest of Henty's early books) takes the reader to the Holy Land at the time of the Third Crusade and the struggle between Richard I and Saladin; *In Freedom's Cause*, a century later, deals with Scotland at the time of Wallace and Bruce.

Henty wrote three books each for the fourteenth and fifteenth centuries: *St. George for England* is really the story of the Black Prince; *A March on London* deals with Wat Tyler's rebellion, while *The Lion of St. Mark*, one of Henty's most popular titles, takes us to Venice. *Both Sides the Border* concerns the very beginning of the fifteenth century and features Glendower and Hotspur, while *At Agincourt* really centres on the White Hoods of Paris, the battle only featuring at the end of the story. Henty then avoids any further involvement in that troubled century as far as English history is concerned, and his third book, *A Knight of the White Cross*, is about the Knights of St. John and the siege of Rhodes.

The sixteenth century is generally regarded as one of the most formative as well as exciting in English history yet Henty does not touch upon a single event under the first four Tudors. He wrote five stories set in this century: *By Right of Conquest* takes us to Mexico under Cortez; *St. Bartholomew's Eve* to France during the Huguenot Wars; *Under Drake's Flag* to adventures in South America and the south seas with little history involved; while *By Pike and Dyke* and *By England's Aid* cover the Dutch wars of independence. It is almost as though Henty did not want to become involved in English history during that century.

The reverse is the case for the seventeenth century. Henty placed seven stories during that period, none of them among his best: two, *The Lion of the North* and *Won by the Sword*, cover events in the Thirty Years' War, and *In the Hands of the Malays* is set in the Dutch East Indies. The other four are set actually in the British Isles: *Friends Though Divided* (one of Henty's weakest stories) is about the Civil War; *When London Burned* deals with the Restoration under Charles II; *John Hawke's Fortune* (a curious short story for younger readers) is about Monmouth's Rebellion; while *Orange and Green* is set in Ireland at the time of the Battle of the Boyne.

Fourteen full-length Hentys are set in the eighteenth century, beginning with *The Cornet of Horse*, *In the Irish Brigade*, *The Bravest of the Brave* and *A Jacobite Exile* which are concerned with the wars that dominated the first fifteen years of the century. *Bonnie*

Prince Charlie and *With Frederick the Great* need no explanation; *Held Fast For England* tells the story of the siege of Gibraltar. Two stories are set in North America—*With Wolfe in Canada* and *True to the Old Flag* (the American War of Independence); three in India—*With Clive in India, The Tiger of Mysore* and *At the Point of the Bayonet* (which takes us into the nineteenth century). Finally, two stories—*In the Reign of Terror* and *No Surrender!* (about the rising in the Vendée)—are placed in revolutionary France.

The remaining forty-two Henty stories are set in the nineteenth century and of these four overlap into the twentieth. This is significant for, although Henty claimed that he hoped to cover all British history as far as its wars were concerned, his interest and knowledge are overwhelmingly in his own century. These forty-two stories divide into the following subjects or areas. Three—*Through the Fray, Facing Death* and *Sturdy and Strong*—concern the English social scene.* Six—*On the Irrawaddy, To Herat and Cabul, Through the Sikh War, In Times of Peril, For Name and Fame* and *A Soldier's Daughter*—are about British India or neighbouring Burma and Afghanistan and very much a part of Henty's development of the imperial theme.† So too are the seven books dealing with Africa—*By Sheer Pluck, The Young Colonists, A Chapter of Adventures, The Dash for Khartoum, With Kitchener in the Soudan, With Buller in Natal* and *With Roberts to Pretoria.*‡ *Through Three Campaigns* is divided between imperial India (two campaigns) and Africa (one) and, taken with the two Boer War stories—*With Buller in Natal* and *With Roberts to Pretoria*, just brings us into the twentieth century. Four stories are about the United States of America—*Captain Bayley's Heir, With Lee in Virginia, Redskin and Cowboy* and *In the Heart of the Rockies.*§

Four more of the nineteenth-century stories have no historical content at all but are simply adventures: *Out on the Pampas* (the first Henty) which is set in the Argentine; *A Final Reckoning*—bush life in Australia; *The Treasure of the Incas*; and *In the Hands of the Cave-Dwellers*—fighting Indians in Mexico.

There remain seventeen books which may be described as historical novels although in one or two cases the historical content

---

* See Chapter twelve.
† See Chapter eight.
‡ See Chapter nine.
§ See Chapter ten.

4

is small. No less than eight of these are set in the Napoleonic Wars, a period much favoured by Henty: *A Roving Commission* and *By Conduct and Courage* have naval backgrounds, *At Aboukir and Acre* deals with Napoleon in Egypt; *The Young Buglers*, *With Moore at Corunna* and *Under Wellington's Command* each concerns a period of the Peninsular War; *Through Russian Snows* covers the retreat from Moscow and *One of the 28th* features the battle of Waterloo. Of the remaining nine stories *With Cochrane the Dauntless* is really adventure in South America with little history attached, *In Greek Waters* has the Greek War of Independence as its background and again contains little real history; *Maori and Settler*, although subtitled 'The New Zealand War', is largely taken up with a tediously long sea journey and settler life, the war being neither central to the story nor especially well-handled when it does occur. Two of the best, as well as two of the earliest, Hentys are *The Young Franc-Tireurs* about the Franco-Prussian War and *Jack Archer* set in the Crimean War. *Condemned as a Nihilist* is a good story with some fine descriptions of Siberia in the latter part of the nineteenth century, *Out with Garibaldi* deals with the freeing of Italy, *With the British Legion* is set in Spain at the time of the Carlist Wars, and *With the Allies to Pekin*, about the Boxer Rising, is the fourth Henty to reach into the twentieth century.

Henty *aficionados* will have their own choices of best and worst from this long list, but some of these books bear unmistakable signs of haste and lack of interest on the part of the author who was clearly only concerned to fulfil his yearly quota of three books: (among these potboilers most people would place *In Greek Waters*, *Through Three Campaigns* and *With the Allies to Pekin*). Some reach a high standard though it is doubtful whether anyone would claim that a Henty boys' story is a memorable example of the genre. On the other hand Henty was a professional and he maintains a consistent level of research into his backgrounds and competent writing.

Henty also wrote a number of short stories, not all for boys, which have been gathered into several collections such as *Yarns on the Beach* which contains 'Do Your Duty', 'Surly Joe' and 'A Fish Wife's Dream'; or *Tales of Daring and Danger* which contains 'Bears and Dacoits', 'The Paternosters', 'A Pipe of Mystery', 'White-Faced Dick' and 'A Brush with the Chinese'. Other Henty stories appeared singly and sometimes concerned women or girls. These include 'Saved by a Woman', 'A Prevision of Evil' and 'Plucky and Cool'. An excellent boys' short story set in the Franco-Prussian War, 'The Spy of Belfort', came out in the November 1883 issue of *Grip*. More obviously adult short stories include 'An Anxious Time' written in a John Buchan 'Peter Pienaar' South African vein; or the delightful (anonymously published) 'Sixty-Eight in Abyssinia'.

Henty also wrote two extensive accounts of the campaigns he followed as a war correspondent in Africa, *The March to Magdala* and *The March to Coomassie*, and eleven full-length adult novels. One of these, *A Woman of the Commune*, also appears as *Cuthbert Hartington* and as *A Girl of the Commune*. The other adult novels are: *A Search for a Secret, All but Lost, Gabriel Allen, M.P., The Curse of Carne's Hold, A Hidden Foe, Rujub the Juggler, Dorothy's Double, The Queen's Cup, Colonel Thorndyke's Secret* and *The Lost Heir*. None, according to the Dictionary of National Biography, achieved much success.*

Apart from his contributions to various boys' magazines, Henty also wrote *Those Other Animals* and two very scarce short stories first published by the Society for Promoting Christian Knowledge: 'The Plague Ship' and 'The Ranche in the Valley'. Finally, at the time of the Diamond Jubilee in 1897, he produced *The Sovereign Reader: Scenes from the Life and Reign of Queen Victoria*.

---

* I have read two of his adult novels, *Rujub the Juggler* and *Gabriel Allen, M.P.* and both have a period charm which I found surprising; Henty's adult novels have, I suspect, been generally underrated.

CHAPTER SEVEN

Henty and History

HENTY WAS NO historian; nor did he ever claim to be one. He was a teacher of history and he used the medium of his boys' stories for that purpose. Above all, he wanted to convey a sense of British greatness and impact: upon Europe, upon the Americas or upon those many lands which were to be incorporated into the British Empire. Henty was primarily concerned with his sense of British greatness, as he saw it, at the time in which he lived, and though his histories might be set in the fourteenth century the heroes, as he often reminded his readers, were endowed with all those qualities of character which supposedly had brought the empire into being, were currently sustaining it and would maintain it in the future.

Those who regard Henty as a teacher of history may be surprised, on reading his books, to discover that he includes hardly any dates, although he would often go to endless lengths, especially in his later books, to provide lists of regimental names, numbers and supply trains engaged in battles. His rejection of the more tiresome minutiae of history no doubt contributed to his popularity in this field. In *Through the Fray*, when the new schoolmaster takes over, 'History was rather a lecture from the master than a repetition of dry facts and dates by the boys'. Henty kept to this formula and, at his best, could make the lecture a stirring descriptive piece. For him, mood was often more important than fact: he wanted to convey the spirit of the times and the general motives which, say, had led the British to fight the French at Agincourt.

There is a much quoted description, by Raymond Blathwayt, of Henty's method of work which appeared in *Great Thoughts from Master Minds* in 1902: 'How Boys' Books are Written'. Only after reading Henty's own evocation of his working method can one appreciate what his historical standing might be.

When I have settled on a period in history I send to the London

Library for ten books specially dealing with that period. I glance through them to see which gives me the kind of information I want, and then I sit down to write without any previous idea whatever of what the story is going to be. It gradually builds itself up from its surroundings. When I get to the purely historical part I have three or four of the books open before me, as I insist particularly that all my history shall be absolutely unassailable. I dictate every word—in that way I think you obtain larger, finer sentences, and I smoke the whole time. My work is extremely rapidly done. On more than one occasion I have completed a book of one hundred and forty thousand words in twenty days.

No one working in that way could claim to be an historian; nor did Henty.

Some critics have implied that Henty was a plagiarist. In a high proportion of his historical tales, though not all, he cites in his preface the authorities on which he has mainly relied. In some cases he quotes more or less verbatim from a source when he is writing a purely historical passage and usually acknowledges his indebtedness—occasionally in the text, more often in the preface. Interestingly, the pace of the historical narrative clearly changes and becomes more vibrant where Henty is especially enamoured of his subject or owes a great deal to a particular source.

Two examples might be taken to illustrate this characteristic. In *The Bravest of the Brave* ('With Peterborough in Spain'), the real hero of the novel is evidently not the lad Jack who is pressed for service in the army and becomes one of the earl's officers, but Peterborough himself: indeed, the book gives a splendid portrait of the eccentric yet brilliant commander whose exploits during the War of the Spanish Succession were second only to those of his more illustrious contemporary, Marlborough, in the north. Henty, too often, appears to be on the side of orthodoxy yet he warms to this difficult man. Thus, in his preface, he says: 'His eccentricities were great; he was haughty and arrogant, hasty and passionate, he denied his God, quarrelled with his king, and rendered himself utterly obnoxious to every party in the state. And yet there was a vast amount of good in this strange man. He was generous and warm-hearted to a fault, kind to those in station beneath him, thoughtful and considerate for his troops, who adored him, cool in danger, sagacious in difficulties, and capable at need of evincing a

patience and calmness wholly at variance with his ordinary impet-
uous character.' In the last sentence of this preface Henty says:
'For the historical events I have described, and for the details of
Peterborough's conduct and character, I have relied chiefly upon
the memoir of the earl written by Mr. C. Warburton.'

Much of the book clearly depends upon Warburton and the story
comes most alive when Peterborough as opposed to the hero is at
the centre of the action. Henty was enchanted by his subject and
the story of Peterborough's astonishing feats and deceptions of the
enemy in Spain as well as the furious antagonism which his brilliance
excited among the allies give the story its chief appeal. The parts
allotted to the young hero are well enough told, yet Henty is most
concerned to provide a picture of a charismatic military commander.

Towards the end of the book, when the earl leaves Spain, Henty
writes: 'It is satisfactory to know that from the moment of the
earl's departure misfortune and disaster fell upon the fortunes of
King Charles, and that the crown which he had received from the
English earl was wrested from his unworthy grasp.' That sentence
provides the reason for much of Henty's success and equally explains
the basis for much of the criticism which can be levelled against his
history: he was unashamedly partisan. He wanted to teach his boy
readers a certain kind, or aspect, of history. This is not to say he
falsified facts; he did not, priding himself upon his accuracy,
although a historian may well fault him in detail. He did want to
show the general greatness of the British people, which he maintains
in the teeth of all their setbacks, so that when he is obliged to recount failures he is unsparing in his censure of those he regards as
responsible.

In *Wulf the Saxon*, the central historical figure is the romantic
and appealing King Harold and his defeat and death at the Battle
of Hastings the climax of the book. In his preface Henty says:
'Although the immediate results of the Battle of Hastings may have
been of less importance to the world than were those of some other
great battles, the struggle has, in the long run, had a greater influence
upon the destiny of mankind than any other similar event that has
ever taken place.' That is a highly debatable statement, but at least
Henty makes such pronouncements unequivocally. The problem
arises with the reader: whereas an adult would be likely to challenge
such a statement or at least query it, a twelve- or thirteen-year-old
would probably accept it as fact and read the story in that light. In

the same preface Henty says of the mixture of races which resulted: 'Moreover, it has helped to produce the race that has peopled Northern America, Australia, and the South of Africa, holds possession of India, and stands forth as the greatest civilizer in the world.' Here again, in a fundamentally biased way, he is dictating to his young readers the viewpoint from which they should proceed; in this sense Henty was a propagandist. Yet he was also a good story-teller, and he maintains a splendid, often thrilling pace in his account of Harold's ill-fated journey to Normandy, when he fell into the hands of William, and the battles of Stamford Bridge and Hastings. He generously acknowledges his source, 'Freeman's magnificent *History of the Norman Conquest of England*, which I hope will be perused by all my older readers should they be able to obtain it'; and, in effect, tells his young readers that, though Harold was a brave and splendidly heroic figure, in the long run England benefited from the Conquest and that the generation for whom he was writing was a product of the mingling of Saxon and Norman.

Henty never undertook original research for his books. When he claimed that his history was all strictly accurate, he meant that he stuck to the main authorities on the particular period with which he was dealing. Sometimes one authority, effectively, gave him all he required—and he acknowledged it; at others his work is the result of reading ten or so books and, though chunks of the history may come from one or other source, Henty was not plagiarizing in the sense in which that word is normally employed. Perhaps his method of work could be compared with that of a history student who, on his tutor's recommendation, consults half a dozen sources for his essay, which subsequently includes many references, quotations and footnotes. Henty merely cut out the references and footnotes.*

In an article published after his death by the *Boys' Own Paper*, Henty says of his historical books:

> The idea of writing historical books first occurred to me in consequence of the success which attended the production of *The Young Franc-Tireurs*, which I wrote on the conclusion of the Franco-German War. I next wrote *The Young Buglers*, a story of the Peninsular War, and the result determined me to stick to historical stories, and if I lived long enough, to treat all the wars

---

* I am indebted to Peter Newbolt for this analogy.

of England. My object has always been to write good history. Of course, to make it go down with the boys it has to be mixed with a very large amount of personal adventure, but I have never permitted myself to deviate in the very slightest degree from historical facts, except where the boy hero is, so to speak, on the loose. That is the reason of the popularity of my books amongst parents.

Henty's early experience in the Crimean War and his twenty years as a war correspondent ensured his subsequent preference for writing about military campaigns. In some of his books about contemporary campaigns—*With Kitchener in the Soudan* or *With Roberts to Pretoria*, for example—it is clearly Henty the war correspondent who takes over and his story is full of details culled from accounts which must have appeared in the press or despatches at the time. In the same posthumous article, Henty says:

'The shortest time in which I ever wrote a book was when I did *With Buller in Natal*. I had not intended to write a story of the war, as I thought it would be too up-to-date. I had already finished my three books [for the year]; they were set up in type and ready to be printed. My publishers, however, urged me to write a war book.

'How long can you give me?' I asked. 'A month', they replied. 'I did it in twenty-four days counting in the Sundays, though I never work on Sundays. The book ran to 140,000 words . . .'

Henty's general history was all of a pattern and with a broad brush he described the advancement of the British people whether fighting the Spanish or French or conquering their later imperial subjects. Often it is the historical footnotes he provides which give his stories their extra fascination and much of this information was of a kind that boys like to store away. In *The Cat of Bubastes*, for example, there occurs the following description of a hen farm in ancient Egypt:

At these places there are long rows of little boxes piled up on each other into a wall five feet high. The door of each of these boxes has a hole in it through which the fowl can put its head, with a little sort of shutter that closes down on it. A fowl is placed in each box. Then the attendants go round two together; one carries a basket filled with little balls of meal, the other lifts the shutter,

and as the fowl puts its head out catches it by the neck, makes it
open its beak, and with his other hand pushes the ball of meal
down its throat . . . Then each time the flap is lifted they think
it is daylight, and pop out their heads at once to see. In about ten
days they get quite fat and plump, and are ready for market.

The weakness in Henty's historical writing when he goes back
into medieval times is simply that he has no feel for the period: his
heroes are always Victorian public-school prefects and his judgements are Victorian too, sounding most odd when they are put into
the mouths of fourteenth- or fifteenth-century characters. Thus in
Both Sides the Border the father of the hero, Oswald, is reconciled
to the fact that his son has learnt to read when later the boy turns
out to be so good at military strategy. He says: 'I am not ashamed
to own when I am wrong; it would not be English or honest not to
do so; reading certainly came in mightily useful there.' This from
a petty border chief who spends his life raiding into Scotland and
stealing cattle or fighting off the avenging Scottish marauders.

In an article which appeared in Bulletin Number 3 of the Henty
Society of March 1978, Terry Corrigan writes of *G. A. Henty as
Military Historian*. He takes up the claim, repeatedly made by Henty,
that his historical details were accurate and then demonstrates in
an analysis of his account of the Battle of Waterloo in *One of the 28th*
the high probability that Henty had his timings wrong. More important, he argues that Henty fails even to mention one of the turning
points in the whole battle when Ney mistakenly launched an attack
because he thought the allied line was crumbling and met instead
unbroken infantry squares. Corrigan then compares the style of
Henty's presentation of a battle scene with that of other writers, to
Henty's detriment, his judgement being that much of Henty's
descriptive historical writing is flat. This indeed is true and
unsurprising considering the author's method of work. When he
found first-class sources (whatever the bias of the actual author may
have been) his historical description is much more lively: when he
failed in his search at the London Library, he did not continue to
burrow away until he found better works of reference. The result
is often one of omission rather than inaccuracy. As Corrigan says
in his conclusion, 'Henty never made any claim to being a military
historian'; he goes on to quote B. McCall Barbour, in the *Boys'
Illustrated Annual* of 1893 that 'Henty is able to invest the dry facts

of history with life, and make them attractive to the modern school-boy, says not a little for his power as a story-teller for boys. It is questionable if history has any better means of fixing itself in the minds of youthful readers than as it is read in the pages of G. A. Henty's works.'

In his preface to *The Young Franc-Tireurs* Henty says: 'Many of the occurrences in this tale are related almost in the words in which they were described to me by those who took part in them, and nearly every fact and circumstance actually occurred according to my own knowledge.' He uses footnotes in this book, a practice he later dropped. At one stage, there is a passage describing a brutal Prussian major who orders his lieutenant to shoot in cold blood some captured peasants who had helped the franc-tireurs. The lieutenant protests and then carries out the order. Afterwards he walks up to the major to report that he has done his duty, then he draws his revolver and shoots himself. This incident is footnoted by Henty: 'An historical fact.'

Henty's prefaces are a mine of information. He uses them to indicate several matters of significance about the ensuing story: first, the degree of importance he attaches to the historical events which are the basis for his story; second, the assertion that all the history is accurate; third, a particular moral that will emerge in the course of the narrative; and fourth, his principal sources.

Sometimes, and more particularly in his earlier novels, Henty will include an historical digression in order to explain something rather than simply using history as part of the story. Thus in *The Cornet of Horse* it is established that the hero, Rupert, is a Tory and there follows an explanation of the original difference between Tory and Whig. Or when Marlborough makes a highly complimentary speech to Rupert's mother, Henty adds: 'Nowadays, such a speech as this would be thought to savour of mockery, but gentlemen two hundred years since ordinarily addressed women in the language of high-flown compliment.' Henty also makes some sweeping historical assertions in this story. Describing the background to the War of the Spanish Succession, he explains why neither Russia nor Italy was involved: 'In fact, with the exception of Russia, still in the depths of barbarism, and Italy, which was then a battle-field rather than a nation, all the states of Europe were ranged on one side or the other.' On the other hand, Henty can clarify the extremely complex causes of the War of the

Spanish Succession, a knack by no means possessed by all historians.

In *The Young Buglers* Henty says baldly that the Siege of Lille was the greatest—'with the exception of that of Sebastopol—that has ever taken place in history . . .' More serious is Henty's habitual practice of making characters think and act out of period. Thus at the end of the story Rupert marries the daughter of a French marquis who delivers himself of the following sentiment: 'After what I have seen of your free England, the despotism of our kings and the feudal power of our nobles disgust me, and I foresee that sooner or later a terrible upheaval will take place.' Allowing for author's licence (and possibly Henty already had in mind *In the Reign of Terror* about the French Revolution), even the most enlightened French nobleman at the time of Marlborough simply would not have thought in such terms. Yet it is a technique Henty uses continually in order to make foreign, and often extremely unlikely, characters express admiration for the British way of doing things; so that his young readers could be pardoned for imagining that the whole world was in a state of more or less fixed admiration of Britain and everything she represented.

In some of his books which are essentially about British history—that is, about internal dissensions between English and Irish or English and Scots—Henty manages a remarkable impartiality. This, for example, is the case in *Friends Though Divided* and *Orange and Green*, both of which feature two friends, one on either side in the struggle. Again, in his story covering the lives of Wallace and Bruce, *In Freedom's Cause*, Henty makes a very strong, almost passionate, case on behalf of the Scots: 'They knew the woes which English domination had brought upon Wales and Ireland; and though as yet without a leader, and at present hopeless of a successful rising, every true Scotchman was looking forward to the time when an attempt might be made to throw off the English yoke.' This is, incidentally, one of the books in which Henty freely refers to his sources in the text. After describing the massacre of Berwick, for example, he says: 'Contemporary accounts differ as to the numbers who perished on this occasion. Langtoff says 4,000; Hingford, 8,000; Knighton, another English writer, 17,000; and Matthew of Westminster, 60,000. Whichever of these writers is correct, it is certain that almost the whole of the men, women, and children of the largest and most populous Scottish town were butchered by the orders of the English King . . .'

At one point, he puts into the mouth of an Irish chief the following words: 'With us it is different. First they conquer all the country; then from a wide tract, a third perhaps of the island, they drive out the whole of the people, and establish themselves firmly there, portioning the land among the soldiery and repeopling the country with an English race.' Indeed, by the end one has read an excellent tract in favour of total independence for both Ireland and Scotland, although that is not what Henty intended. He corrects the impression in a later book about Scotland, *Bonnie Prince Charlie*, in which he takes the orthodox view of the prince and the end of Stuart hopes: 'Happily the rising of '45 was the last effort on behalf of the Stuarts. Scotland accepted the decision as final, and the union between the two countries became close and complete. Henceforth Scotchmen went no longer to fight in the armies of France, but took service in that of their own country . . .' In these particular books, Henty seems to be leaning over backwards to be fair to the minority, defeated groups—the Scots and Irish—in order to reconcile them (and his readers) to the fact that they had been incorporated into Great Britain.

Some of Henty's best history is to be found in those stories where he detaches his hero from involvement in an English-dominated setting and, instead, lets him serve with, say, Gustavus Adolphus or Charles XII of Sweden. In *The Lion of the North*, the history is sound and the reader absorbs a great many facts about the terrible wars of religion: that, for instance, at the commencement of the conflict the population of Bohemia was 3,000,000 living in 738 towns and 34,700 villages, while at its close there were only 780,000 people living in 230 towns and 6,000 villages; or, quite another matter, that the English and German languages were much closer to one another than in Henty's time.

It would have made better sense, and been historically more convincing, had Henty made his hero following Gustavus Adolphus a Swede, but here the author faced a different problem which he explains in the posthumous *Boys' Own Paper* article: 'Of course, the hero must be British. That boys will have this so is evident from the fact that the sale of *The Cat of Bubastes*, *The Destruction of Jerusalem* [re-titled *For the Temple*], and *The Young Carthaginian*, in none of which could I possibly place a British boy, has been smaller than that of any books I have written; and they are the three stories that I rather expected would do especially well.' Henty's comment is

interesting for these three are, as he rightly thought, among his best
written stories, achieving a fast pace and a nice balance between the
background history and the adventures of the heroes. Indeed,
precisely because the setting is so removed from Britain, it is as
though he forgets some of his preoccupations with British greatness
and simply gets on with a sound historical novel.

Sometimes Henty makes claims which he does not fulfil. In his
preface to *The Dragon and the Raven*, he describes King Alfred as the
first great Englishman with outstanding qualities, and says, 'And
yet few English boys know more than a faint outline of the events
of Alfred's reign,' Shortly thereafter, he adds: 'In this story I have
tried to supply the deficiency.' In fact he does no such thing. For
once Henty's general clarity of style and ability to explain complicated issues is, understandably, defeated when he attempts to make
plain the intricacies of royal claims:

> Ethelbald received Wessex, the principal part of the kingdom, and
> Ethelwulf took Kent, which he had already ruled over in the time
> of his father Egbert. Ethelwulf died a few months afterwards,
> leaving Kent to Ethelbert, his second surviving son. The follow-
> ing year, to the horror and indignation of the people of the
> country, Ethelbald married his stepmother Judith, but two years
> afterwards died, and Ethelbert, King of Kent, again united
> Wessex to his own dominions, which consisted of Kent, Surrey
> and Sussex. Ethelbert reigned but a short time, and at his death
> Ethelred, his next brother, ascended the throne. Last year
> Alfred, the youngest brother, married Elswitha, the daughter of
> Ethelred Mucil, Earl of Gaini, in Lincolnshire, whose mother
> was one of the royal family of Mercia . . .

It is surprising how often Henty, in spite of his abiding prejudices
about British greatness, could produce an impartial picture of a
figure whom many historians had painted as a monster. In his book
about the French Revolution, *In the Reign of Terror*, he presents an
unusually fair portrait of Robespierre. In *Beric the Briton* his
evocation of Nero is equally balanced. Apart from dealing with the
accusation that Nero fired Rome—'Nero, who had been absent,
reached Rome on the third day of the fire. The accusation that he
had caused it to be lighted, brought against him by his enemies
years afterwards, was absurd'—he puts into the mouth of Beric,
the hero, the following description:

'I am one of Nero's guards, and I do not want to have to hate my work, or to wish well to those from whom I am bound to protect him. To me he is kind and friendly. At times when I am with him in the garden or alone in his room he talks to me as an equal, of books and art, the condition of the people, and other topics . . . It seems to me that there are two Neros: the one a man such as he was when he ascended the throne—gentle; inclined to clemency; desirous of the good of his people, and of popularity; a lover of beautiful things; passionately devoted to art in all its branches; taking far greater pleasure in the society of a few intimate friends than in state pageants and ceremonies. There is another Nero; of him I will not talk. I desire, above all things, not to know him . . .'

Although Henty propounded to an absurd degree the greatness of Britain, he also did not hesitate to pass scathing judgements upon individual historical figures whether he was writing of Queen Elizabeth I or of a near contemporary such as General Elphinstone in Afghanistan. In *St. Bartholomew's Eve*, he says of Elizabeth:

Elizabeth baffled both friends and enemies by her vacillations and duplicity, and her utter want of faith, doling out aid in the spirit of a huckster rather than a queen, so that she was in the end even more hated by the Protestants of Holland and France than by the Catholics of France and Spain.

To those who look only at the progress made by England during the reign of Elizabeth—thanks to her great ministers, her valiant sailors and soldiers, long years of peace at home, and the spirit and energy of her people,—Elizabeth may appear a great monarch. To those who study her character from her relations with the struggling Protestants of Holland and France, it will appear that she was, although intellectually great, morally one of the meanest, falsest, and most despicable of women.

On the whole there are no half-measures about Henty when he decides to condemn. More usually, however, he accepts the standard historical judgements of his time. Of Charles II, who appears in *When London Burned*, he presents a balanced enough picture, bringing out the twin aspects of his character: indecisiveness and ability to act, courage and laziness, brains when aroused to use them offset by a general pleasure-loving indolence. He can also paint an appealingly heroic portrait as with Marshal Ney during the retreat from Moscow in *Through Russian Snows*.

Sometimes the promise is simply not fulfilled. This is the case with Alfred in *The Dragon and the Raven*; and again in *With Cochrane the Dauntless*. In his preface Henty compares Cochrane with Peterborough: 'Both accomplished marvels, and neither was appreciated at his full value by his countrymen, both having a touch of originality that amounted in the case of Peterborough to absolute eccentricity.' Cochrane's long and difficult career evidently appealed to Henty as did Peterborough's, but he never succeeds in bringing Cochrane alive—perhaps he simply could not find ten good books upon Cochrane in the London Library—and the result is a fair adventure story which little more than touches upon Cochrane's achievements in South America and his part in the independence of Chile, Peru and Brazil.

A curious aspect of Henty, who loved the sea and lived in an age when the Royal Navy was the glory of Britain, is that hardly any of his books deal with major naval engagements such as Trafalgar. In *By England's Aid* he dwells at length upon the unpreparedness of the English fleet at the time of the Armada and blames Elizabeth's niggardliness, saying that the great nobles rather than the treasury had to bear half the costs of the fleet, a deliberate aspect of policy he appears to misunderstand. In *A Chapter of Adventures* he describes the naval bombardment of Alexandria, and there is a description of the naval action at Harfleur in *At Agincourt*; minor sea engagements are described in *With Cochrane the Dauntless*, while in *By Conduct and Courage* ('A Story of the Days of Nelson'), whose sub-title might lead the reader to expect the description of a major Nelson engagement, we get instead a curious Henty invention when his hero falls in with Nelson and they are lost in the fog and both briefly captured in Corsica. Only in a short story—'Do Your Duty'—is one of the classic naval engagements, that of Parker and Nelson at the Battle of Copenhagen, a major feature. It is almost as though Henty, who in fact knew so much of the sea, felt inhibited from writing about it because he regarded himself as an amateur.

Despite all criticism, however, Henty succeeded in exciting in his youthful readers an interest in the past that has been achieved by few other writers of juvenile fiction. For that, if nothing else, he has earned a secure place in the pantheon of minor Victorians.

CHAPTER EIGHT

The Indian Stories

HENTY'S INDIAN STORIES, more even than his late African ones, were his justification for empire. He emerges clearly from their pages as an imperial propagandist. He tells the history of British expansion and control over the Indian sub-continent; he also, again and again, makes plain his sense of British superiority in the Indian context and thus of the benefits to be derived by Indians from the imperial presence.

India, in any case, dominated Victorian imperial thinking from the trauma of the Mutiny to Disraeli's triumphant purchase of forty per cent of the shares in the Suez Canal which, effectively, gave control of this 'lifeline' of Empire to Britain. Five of Henty's boys' stories are about India: *With Clive In India*, *The Tiger of Mysore*, *At the Point of the Bayonet*, *Through the Sikh War* and *In Times of Peril*, between them covering the century of expansion from Clive to the Mutiny. One of the best of Henty's adult novels—*Rujub the Juggler*—is also set in India at the time of the Mutiny. Three more stories deal with expansion from the borders of India: *On the Irrawaddy* (the first Burmese War), *To Herat and Cabul* (the first Afghan War), and *For Name and Fame* (the Second Afghan War); two of the campaigns in the story *Through Three Campaigns* concern the North-West Frontier at the turn of the century, as does *A Soldier's Daughter*, while several of his short stories are also set in India. These books provide the historical framework of British expansion in and from India between 1750 and 1900. The historical accounts are good enough and Henty's often ruthless condemnation of incompetent or inadequate British policies or leadership might well in a more subtle context be seen as a deliberate brainwashing technique, since by demonstrating impartiality over the good and bad qualities of British and Indian alike he makes his ultimate message—that the British presence in India was good for India—all the more effective.

In his preface to *With Clive in India* Henty states that he is mainly concerned with history and quotes the sources he has used. The format of the book is the same as ever: the young hero, Charlie Marryat, has lost his father; his uncle obtains a writership for him with the East India Company. During the voyage out a Company doctor explains to Charlie and his friend Peters some of the background to what was then happening in India. Then after adventures at sea including a brush with privateers they arrive in Madras and the two young friends begin their lives in India.

Clive soon appears on the scene and the book at once plunges into the siege of Arcot. In the form of light relief, however, there is the almost Kiplingesque soldier-servant character, Charlie's man, Tim Kelly:

A few days later Tim Kelly came in. 'Plase, yer honours, there's a little shrivelled atomy of a man outside as wants to spake wid ye. He looks for all the world like a monkey wrapped up in white clothes, but he spakes English after a fashion, and has brought this letter for you. The cratur scarce looks like a human being, and I misdoubt me whether you had better let him in.'

'Nonsense, Tim,' Charlie said, opening the letter; 'it's the moonshee we are expecting from Madras. He has come to teach us the native language.'

'Moonshine, is it! by Jabers, and it's a mighty poor compliment to the moon to call him so. And is it the language you're going to larn now. Shure, Mr. Charles, I wouldn't demane myself by larning the lingo of these black hathens. Isn't it for them to larn the English, and mighty pleased they ought to be to get themselves to spake like Christians.'

'But who's going to teach them, Tim?'

'Oh, they larn fast enough,' said Tim. 'You've only got to point to a bottle of water, or to the fire, or whatever else you want, and swear at them, and they understand directly. I've tried it myself over and over again.'

Henty has got the attitude of the common soldier right then and for generations to come.

At one point in the story the hero ponders: 'They are wonderfully clever and ingenious. Look what rough tools that man is working with, and what delicate and intricate work he is turning out. If these fellows could but fight as well as they work, and were but

united among themselves, not only should we be unable to set foot
in India, but the emperor, with the enormous armies which he
would be able to raise, would be able to threaten Europe . . . I can't
make it out. These Sepoys, after only a few weeks training, fight
almost as well as our own men.' Such a reflexion, with its appreciation of Indian qualities, makes imminent British control the more
awe-inspiring for the intelligent young reader.

Henty describes at length the deceptions practised by Clive and
the English upon Omichund as well as their own greed and venality
and says: 'The history of these intrigues is the most unpleasant
feature in the life of Clive . . . Never did an English officer make such
a bargain for himself. But even this is not the most dishonourable
feature of the transaction . . .' Towards the end of the book Charlie
and Peters reflect that they will be sorry to leave the Indian soldiers
when they return to England and then a bit of racial-imperial
propaganda is inserted: 'It is singular that, contemptible as are
these natives of India when officered by men of their own race and
religion, they will fight to the death when led by us.'

The Tiger of Mysore ('A Story of the War with Tippoo Saib')*
is the second historical book about the Company in the Carnatic
and includes one or two features that belie the Henty stereotype.
In the first place the hero's mother is half Indian so that he has
what Victorians referred to as 'a touch of the tarbrush' although he
behaves and speaks entirely like an English boy. His father, a seaman,
has been wrecked off India and his mother is convinced that he is
alive and in one of Tippoo's prisons. She brings the boy up to be
manly and skilled in all qualities he might require in rescuing his
father. She also teaches him to speak like a native. Henty says of the
hero's mother: 'Mrs. Holland was a half-caste, the daughter of an
English woman who had married a young rajah.' Quarter-caste the
boy may be but well-connected for all that. When Dick is fifteen
they set off for India; his mother instructs him most sensibly: 'Say
nothing about my having been born in India, or that my father was
a native rajah. Some of these officials—and still more, their wives—
are very prejudiced, and consider themselves to be quite different
beings to the natives of the country.'

---

* The only allusion Henty ever makes to an unmentionable subject, homo-
sexuality, occurs in sufficiently opaque form in this book: 'Some of the boys,
drummer-boys, or ship's-boys, or little ship's officers, were kept in the Palace
and trained as singers and dancers for Tippoo's amusement.'

At one point in the story, Dick's Indian companion tells an old Hindoo that the killing of the tiger which has earned them both positions with Tippoo was really all Dick's doing. The old man says: 'This is how it is the English have become lords of so wide a territory. They are quick: while we hesitate and spend great time in making up our minds to do anything, they decide and act in a moment; they are always ready, we are always slow; they see the point where a blow has to be struck, they make straight to it and strike. The English Sahib is very young, and yet to him comes in a moment what is the best thing to be done.' Any of Henty's 'dear lads' reading this and similar passages must have seen why the Empire was so extensive.

The book also includes one of the funnier Henty descriptions of burgeoning young love. Dick discovers that an English girl is a captive of Tippoo; she meets him secretly and he resolves to spirit her away when he and his friend Surajah escape from Tippoo's service. Surajah asks if he intends to take the girl and so increase their difficulties. 'Of course I am,' Dick said heartily. 'You don't suppose that an Englishman would be so base as to leave a young countrywoman in the hands of these wretches?' There is little of the half-caste about our Dick.

They escape—the girl is fourteen—and after a long ride: 'Oh, you are good, Dick!' she sighed softly. 'Only to think of your carrying me like this for five hours, without waking me.' Whatever Dick thinks—in the line of duty—it is clear the girl has a crush on him. Brought up in a harem from the age of six Annie's education is somewhat limited, and Dick tells her she will have to learn things such as geography and proceeds to give her some instruction—they are still on horseback going hell for leather—ending his lesson with the sound social advice: 'If you don't know about these things, you can't follow what people are talking about.' Later during the escape Annie, not surprisingly, breaks down. 'Dick looked at her helplessly. A girl in tears was a creature wholly beyond his experience . . .' And when she thanks him for saving her, Dick replies: 'Nonsense, child! I have done what everyone would do if they found a little countrywoman in distress.'

When Dick and Surajah return to Dick's uncle, the rajah, they have to recount all their adventures. At the end the rajah says to his two sons: 'See this . . . here you have proof of the advantages of the training your cousin has had . . . We in India have courage; but it is because our princes and nobles are brought up in indolence and luxury that the English, though but a handful in point of numbers, have become masters of such wide territories.' The rajah goes on to extol the benefits of an English education.

The next Indian novel, *At the Point of the Bayonet* ('A Tale of the Mahratta War') is one of Henty's most imperial stories. In his preface he says: 'The jealousies of the great Mahratta leaders Holkar and Scindia, who were constantly at war with each other, or with the Peishwa at Poona, greatly facilitated our operations, and enabled us, although at the cost of much blood, to free a large portion of India from a race that was a scourge—faithless, intriguing and crafty, cruel, and reckless of life.' There in a nutshell is imperial justification: the civilization brought by the British, moreover, replacing one of the racial stereotypes the Victorians so easily produced and Henty so readily employed in his writings.

At the beginning of the story the hero is rescued from a Mahratta massacre by his faithful Indian nurse—he is a baby in arms—and she brings him up secretly as an Indian (though so accomplished and far-sighted is she that she also teaches him English against the day when he will want to resume his own nationality). This contrivance enables the boy to speak fluent Mahratti and, with the benefit of dye, pass anywhere as a native. After the massacre, when the nurse reaches her brother's home, he asks her how she has liked being among the English:

> 'I liked it very well,' the woman said. 'They are very kind and considerate to nurses, and although they get angry when the gorrawallah or other men neglect their duty, they do not punish them as a Mahratta master would do. They are not double-faced; when they say a thing they mean it, and their word can always be trusted. As a people, no doubt, they are anxious to extend their dominion, but they do not wish to do so for personal gain. They are not like the princes here, who go to war to gain territory and revenue . . .'

The device of making the native praise the imperial British works well. The sentiments expressed are retrospective ones personifying the high Victorian idea of trust but hardly the prevailing attitude at the time in which the story takes place. Henty might have recalled the famous remark Clive made at his trial when questioned about the fortune he had amassed while in the service of the company;

he replied that in retrospect he was astonished by his own modera-
tion. This form of special pleading, represented here by the nurse's
eulogy of the British and their motives, is an excellent example of
Henty's technique.

Several times in this story Henty makes someone predict that the
English will rule all India: this is a perfectly justifiable device and
gives greater authenticity and verisimilitude to events. Other devices
are not so convincing. The nurse, for example, is an unlikely woman:
wise beyond her station and apparently more knowledgeable about
Britain (so that she may pass the information on to her adopted
charge) than she could reasonably be expected to be. When as a
young man Harry, the hero, goes to a British Resident and tells his
extraordinary story the Resident at once believes him: 'I can the
more readily believe it, inasmuch as, in spite of your colour [Harry
is dyed], I can perceive a certain likeness to Major Lindsay [Harry's
father], whom I knew intimately.'

Despite having been brought up as a Mahratta Harry is deeply
imbued with an appreciation of the benefits that would come from
the extension of British rule in India: 'But if in the future the
British become the masters of India, the Mahrattas will have no
reason to regret having given them a foothold. Wherever their
powers extend, the natives are far better off than they were under the
rule of their own princes. Were the British masters, there would be
no more wars, no more jealousies, and no more intrigues; the
peasants would till their fields in peace, and the men who now take
to soldiering would find more peaceful modes of earning a living.'

Harry goes off to Malaya and actually obtains the agreement for
the eventual cession of Singapore Island. The racial stereotypes
continue: 'The treacherous nature of the Malays was well known.'
There are unintentional ironies in Henty when he has to reconcile
his stereotypes with imperial advance. Thus of the Andaman
Islanders he first says: 'The natives of the Andaman Islands are
among the lowest types of humanity known.' Later, however,
referring to their hostility to anyone who attempts to land on their
territory, he also makes someone say: 'One can hardly blame them
for their hostility. Naturally, they want to have the place to themselves, and are just as averse to our landing as our forefathers were
to Julius Caesar and his Romans . . . Of course they would be, if
they only knew it, very much better off by being civil. We have
numbers of things that would be invaluable to them. For instance,

I would willingly give them a dozen cooking-pots and as many frying-pans if they would let us obtain water peaceably.'

On the Irrawaddy ('A Story of the First Burmese War') covers part of the middle period of British imperial activity on the Indian sub-continent. The benefits of British rule are of course strongly advocated throughout this book and the hero is very much in the mould of a late Victorian district officer.

Of the war Henty says: 'It was undertaken without any due comprehension of the difficulties to be encountered from the effects of climate and the deficiency of transport; the power and still more the obstinacy and arrogance of the Court of Ava were altogether underrated . . .' Later he adds: 'No worse government has ever existed than that of Burma when, with the boast that she intended to drive the British out of India, she began the war; no people were ever kept down by a more grinding tyranny, and the occupation of the country by the British has been an even greater blessing to the population than has that of India.' So much for the Burmese!

The hero, Stanley Brooke, is left fatherless at sixteen but with an uncle in trade in Burma; having lived for years in barracks in India he has become fluent in several native languages. Describing how the Burmese cause trouble for the British, Stanley's uncle says: 'With such ignorant people there is but one argument understood, namely, force; and sooner or later we shall have to give them such a hearty thrashing that they will be quiet for some time. Still, I grant that the difficulties are great. Their country is a tremendous size, the beggars are brave . . .'

Stanley takes part in the campaign, is captured, escapes and then, as he makes his way through the Burmese jungle, he fearlessly attacks a leopard when he comes upon it crouching over two men it has downed. He kills it and rescues one of the two who turns out to be a bandit and subsequently becomes Stanley's devoted follower and servant. The tale of this exceptionally daring exploit naturally leaks out and follows Stanley all through the story. The bandits, amongst whom Stanley spends some time, understandably are astonished that he should have risked his life for a total stranger:

'One life is all a man has,' the Burman said. 'Why should he give it for a stranger?'

'I don't think that we stop to think of that,' Stanley said; 'it seems to us natural that if we see another in danger of his life, we should try to save it, whether it is a man or woman, whether it be from fire or from any other fate.'

Later Meinik, the bandit, gives Stanley a bag of rubies. They have been stolen—but: 'Stanley felt that he could not refuse a gift so offered, even though the goods were stolen.' They help to found his and his uncle's fortunes.

When Stanley explains that the possible outcome of the war will be British rule, Meinik says philosophically: 'I think that would be good for us.' Later, Stanley has no doubts: 'I am sure that it would be a good thing for them, Meinik. The people of India are a great deal better off under us than they were under their native rulers . . .'

Henty somewhat spoils his arguments about the benefits that British rule will bring to Burma when he discusses the position of Siam: 'But our occupation of several points on the coast of Tenasserim roused the fears of Siam, and inclined it to the belief that we might prove an even more dangerous neighbour than Burma.' Attitudes towards native peoples abound in this book: 'It may be all very well to be lenient when one is dealing with a European enemy, but magnanimity does not pay when you have to do with Orientals, who don't care a rap for treaty engagements, and who always regard concessions as being simply proof of weakness.' So do the stereotypes: 'While those whose houses had been burned set to work, with a cheerfulness characteristic of their race. . . .'

Halfway through *On the Irrawaddy* the reformed bandit, Meinik, has become what may only be described as a good native:

'Burmese are great fools,' he often said to Stanley. 'They think they know a great deal; they know nothing at all. They think they are great fighters; they are no good at fighting, for one Englishman beats ten of them. Their government is no good— it keeps everyone very poor and miserable. You come here; you know nothing of the country, and yet you make everyone comfortable. We ride through the villages; we see everyone rejoicing that they are governed by the English, and hoping that the English will never go away again.'

Stanley has to dispense justice in conquered areas and acts for a time just like a district officer. He demotes one village headman for malpractices and warns him that if he appeals to the general—who will have had Stanley's report: 'I can tell you that the general, when he reads it, will be much more likely to order you a sound flogging than to reinstate you in your office.'

The latter half of the story concerns Stanley's rescue of his cousin, another Brooke, who has been captured. When eventually Stanley rescues Harry and the latter attempts to thank him, Stanley replies: 'You had better say nothing about it, Harry; I have only done what you would have done had you been in my place; had you been in charge of that party, and I had been carried off, I know you would have done all in your power to rescue me.' So far so good, but then Stanley adds: 'You might not have succeeded quite so well, because you do not know their language, but I know that you would have tried. After all, I have not run anything like so much risk as I did when I rescued Meinik from the leopard. And he, of course, was an absolute stranger to me.' There is a piety about Henty's heroes (apart from their penchant for drawing attention to their deeds) which is positively nauseating. Eventually, the rescue completed, Stanley leaves the Burmese village: 'It had been something altogether new to them to have officials among them who paid for everything. These Englishmen had treated them kindly, and were pleased and contented with everything.' When Meinik gets to Calcutta with Stanley, he again philosophizes: 'The Burmese are fools, master; they should have sent two or three men here before they made up their minds to go to war. If they had been truly told what Calcutta was like, they would never have ventured to make war with the English.'

To Herat and Cabul ('A Story of the First Afghan War') is one of the best Henty mixtures of history and a good yarn. The first Afghan War in any case was a dramatic affair and the annihilation of the British army in the pass down from Cabul one of the great disasters of the Victorian era; so that, even in 1902 when the story appeared, it would be an event still talked about if not remembered.

Henty does not spare the commander, Elphinstone, though he makes plain that he was far too old and should never have been given the command; he also says more than once that it was an unjust war on the British side and is scathing in his denunciations of Macnaghten, the Political Officer, who was largely responsible for it. 'Unhappily the general was old and infirm, incapable of decision of any kind, and in his imbecile hands the troops, who in October could have met the whole forces of Afghanistan in fight, were kept inactive while the Afghans pillaged the stores with the provisions for the winter, and insulted and bearded them in every way.'

By this stage in his writing Henty was a convinced apologist for empire and frequently puts into the mouths of his native characters such sentiments as the following: 'We all love and respect the English. They have always been our good friends, and glad indeed should we be were they masters here as they are in India; for I have been there, and know how just is their rule—how they oppress no one, and will not suffer others to do so. This would be a happy city indeed if your people were our masters.' In retrospect little changes: 'I am merely fighting for England, for it is of the utmost importance that the gate of India should not be in the hands of Persia, especially if, as you say, Russian influence is dominant in Teheran.'

Henty may have been an imperialist; he was also (unlike many of his countrymen then and since) sensitive to local customs: 'Father always impressed upon me that we were strangers in this part of the world, and must be very cautious not to show any aversion to its customs. It would lead us into endless trouble if we were to show in any way that what to them seems only natural, was to us revolting.'

There is an implicit dishonesty in some of the courses adopted by Henty's heroes, perhaps not always recognized by the author himself. Thus at one point in this story the hero, Angus, is being spied upon and his faithful follower, Azim, wants to surprise the man and knife him—a perfectly proper sentiment. Angus, however, tells Azim:

'If he found us escaping and attacked us, we could kill him, Azim, but it is not an Englishman's way to kill men, except in fight.'
Azim shook his head. To his mind this was very foolish.

In the event, forbidden to use his knife, Azim comes up behind the spy and clubs him over the head; he strikes so hard that he kills the man anyway. Angus, though 'tut tutting', is happy to take advantage of the dirty work being done for him. They search the dead man and find gold on him which Angus tells his follower to keep: it is your spoil, he says, thus absolving himself. Victorian morality over accepting presents might be described as shrewd: 'Angus saw that, offered as it was, he should greatly hurt the Afghan's feelings if he refused the immense ruby surrounded by diamonds that Dost Mahomed had sent him.'

Through the Sikh War ('A Tale of the Conquest of the Punjaub')

comes next in the Indian sequence. It is a curiosity of Henty the
historian that he often fails to date the period he is describing: thus
in his preface to this story he says of the wars which won India for
the empire—'few, if any, were more brilliant and hard fought than
those which terminated in the annexation of the Punjaub'. Whether
he felt his young readers either should know the dates or that it
would be a good exercise for them to find out is not clear.

The hero, Percy, is left fatherless at fifteen but his uncle, an
adventurer in the service of Runjeet Singh, the Sikh prince, invites
him out to his fortified castle in the Punjaub. Like all Henty's
heroes (it is a device to ensure subsequent exciting adventures in
disguise as well as advice) Percy has learnt some Hindu at school,
and on the ship out he learns Punjaubi.

The uncle has married a Sikh woman. He says of the Sikhs that,
while they will fight pluckily enough, they need English officers to
discipline and lead them: ' . . . but they would be worth very little
if deprived of their European officers.'

Percy soon leaves his uncle, who is a heroic figure in his own right,
to enter the service of the Company and have adventures of his
own. Henty makes the point that the habit of victory for the British
was fundamental (at least in the nineteenth century) so that the
troops are not at all dismayed at the power of the Sikhs or their
warlike reputation.

Yet again there appears the subservient pro-English native: 'I
would rather have a native prince; but far better than the nominal
rule of a boy, protected by foreign bayonets, would be the rule of
the foreigners themselves, for they, at least, can make the law
respected, punish ill-doers, and preserve peace and order.' Such
sentiments simply do not come from peasants in any society which
is on the brink of being taken over by the invading forces of another
people. It is a Henty contrivance which is both irritating and un-
historical.

Henty well reflects the arrogance of a people assured that they
are right and will succeed. Thus the young Percy says to a rajah
who has determined to fight the Company: 'Were the Sikh nation
ten times as numerous as they are, the end would be the same.'
What he means is British rule.

In Times of Peril is about the Indian Mutiny. Few events in
Victoria's reign excited such emotions in Britain as the Mutiny and
Henty's treatment accords with the general sentiment:

For they were excited by the thought that in a few hours they would be with friends, once more soldiers instead of fugitives, with power to fight in defence of their sovereign's dominions, and of the helpless women and children exposed to the fury of the atrocious mutineers.

They knew, too, that in acting as they had done, they were performing their duty; and that at a moment when the fate of British India trembled in the balance, the place of every soldier was by the side of the British troops who still maintained the old flag flying in the face of increasing enemy numbers.

Describing British heroism outside Delhi, Henty narrates the death of a young subaltern:

> . . . and said, with a smile, to an old school friend who came in to bid him farewell—
> 'Well, old fellow, *Dulce et decorum est pro patria mori*, and you see it's my case.'

Later, on a different note, he has an English officer say: 'That's sickened them for the present. I expect they'll do nothing till it gets a bit cooler, for even a nigger could hardly stand this.' The relief of Lucknow forms a substantial part of the story.

For Name and Fame ('Through Afghan Passes') is the last of Henty's full-length books centred upon India. Here he is concerned with what Kipling immortalized as the 'Great Game'. In his preface Henty says: 'Afghanistan stands as a dividing line between the two great empires of England and Russia, and it is certain, sooner or later, to become the scene of a tremendous struggle between these nations; possibly the struggle may have begun before these pages are read by you.'

The story is about Roberts in Afghanistan when, during the 1870s and 1880s, Britain saw Russian intrigues there as a threat to her Indian Empire. Henty indulges in classic imperialist sentiments about Afghan soldiers: 'Their weakness consists in their want of organization, their tribal jealousies, and their impatience of regular habits, and of the restraint necessary to render them good soldiers. But when led and organized by English officers there are no better soldiers in the world . . .' Later again: 'Guided by British advice, led by British officers, and, it may be, paid by British gold, Afghanistan is likely to prove an invaluable ally to us when the day comes that Russia believes herself strong enough to move forward towards the goal of all her hopes and efforts for the last fifty years, the conquest of India.'

Will, the hero, after many adventures, is made an officer by General Roberts and recommended for the V.C. The Second Afghan War is well described and Henty produces a number of his usual strictures upon the habits of the native people: 'The disgrace of a broken promise is not one which weighs heavily upon an Afghan's mind, and it is not probable that the thought of his tarnished honour troubled him in the slightest degree . . .'

Two-thirds of *Through Three Campaigns* (possibly Henty's worst book) is devoted to India, dealing first with the Chitral and then the Tirah campaign. Tribute is paid to the 'fidelity and bravery of our Sikh soldiers'; otherwise defending the frontiers of empire is simply accepted as a part of the imperial legacy.

A Soldier's Daughter is a curiosity, a long short story with a heroine, Nita, instead of a boy hero. She is the daughter of Major Ackworth stationed on the North-West Frontier. Nita is in all respects a tomboy: she likes games, can shoot and ride like a man and is averse to all normal female accomplishments. She tells her father she wishes she had been a boy, to which he replies that he rather wished so too. In his description of her talk with her father, Henty demonstrates a sense of humour about the boy-girl situation that is often lacking in his standard formula books for boys. Nita's father has even allowed her to learn to box which seems a bit much even for an eccentric man on the North-West Frontier.

The father goes off with most of the troops, leaving only one officer, Lieutenant Carter, in charge. At once Nita notices that the natives are all disappearing and at her suggestion Carter doubles the guards, now convinced that a feint has drawn off the Major so that the station can be attacked.

Carter admits to this slip of a girl that her brain has worked quicker than his, but she modestly says she will serve under him in the coming emergency. There is then a curious passage in which Carter gives Nita a lesson about the armies of the world: no other nation enjoys fighting as much as Britain; the Germans, though good soldiers, only fight well because of the habit of obedience; the French for nearly the same reason and, he thinks, the Russians also. The Turk likes fighting and is a religious fanatic; the Indians seem imbued with their English masters' love of fighting; the Sikhs,

Punjaubis and Ghoorkhas are, however, equalled by Britain's African subjects, the Hausas.

To all this Nita says very sensibly of the British: 'I expect it is because we have the feeling that we always win our battles.' Carter agrees and then launches into an attack upon the new school-boards which train boys to despise their fathers' artisan callings, preparing them instead to go into petty clerkships or shops. None the less he expects they would all volunteer if there were to be a serious war with France or Germany. Since the Fashoda incident, he does not believe that France would want to fight England but supposes that the Germans might, although this supposition is counterbalanced by the fact that they and the Russians hate each other. Carter finishes this passage, in which he acts as mouthpiece for Henty's prejudices as well as his ideas about the strength of the great powers: 'No, the next war, when it comes, may be between us and Russia; and as it is certain that the little Japs would join us, I think that between us we should make things pretty hot for her.'

The station is duly attacked: Nita first helps in the hospital, but at the end dons one of Carter's uniforms, cuts her hair so that she looks like a boy, and joins the fray. They are taken prisoner. In this dire emergency Carter, though slow-witted, comes up to scratch; Nita is surprised at his firmness and obeys him.

Nita is treated as a boy by her Afridi captors; she escapes, rescues Carter and then for weeks they wander in the hills evading pursuit. When in a tight corner, the peculiar Carter always consults Nita as to their best course of action and she always has the answers. They eventually get back to the regiment and the Major who had so foolishly gone off is delighted to find his daughter is alive. Carter has taken map notes which help his promotion, Nita goes back to England to finish her education but returns three years later to marry Carter. The reader has no doubts as to who will wear the trousers.

CHAPTER NINE

The African Stories

HENTY WROTE SEVEN full-length boys' books about Africa; in addition one of the three episodes from *Through Three Campaigns* is set on that continent. These stories have a particular interest since they cover events which occurred during the last twenty years of the nineteenth century actually while Henty was engaged as a full-time writer. Each book deals with an historical episode which was, effectively, part of the Scramble for Africa, so that Henty's treatment of them exactly reflects Victorian Tory attitudes. Henty also wrote two extended accounts of expeditions he followed as a war correspondent—*The March to Magdala* and *The March to Coomassie*—but only in the latter case did he use the material as background for subsequent boys' stories.

The Africa stories cover the following events: *A Chapter of Adventures* (the bombardment of Alexandria in 1882); *The Dash for Khartoum* (the expedition to relieve Gordon, 1884–1885); *With Kitchener in the Soudan* (Omdurman, 1898); *By Sheer Pluck* (the Gold Coast, 1873–1874); *Through Three Campaigns* (Gold Coast again, the Ashanti War, 1900–1901); *The Young Colonists* (the Zulu War of 1879 and the first Anglo-Boer War of 1881); *With Buller in Natal* and *With Roberts to Pretoria* (the Boer War, 1899–1902).

Henty's reactions in these books are important for two reasons: his comments upon the handling of the campaigns and political situations which were very much before the public mind at the time (and here he writes as a war correspondent rather than as an historian); and his racial and imperial attitudes which in the 1980s read interestingly especially in relation to the Boers in South Africa. African campaigns at the end of the nineteenth century marked the high point of Victorian imperial expansion; Henty makes plain to his young readers that he believes such expansion to be fully justified.

A Chapter of Adventures is almost a non-story and bears evidence of haste on Henty's part, no doubt so that he could fulfil his contract quota for the year. It was produced in 1890 and, despite the sub-title, the bombardment of Alexandria does not form the central part of the book; the real hero in this case is the sea.

After a number of adventures Jack, the hero and by then a midshipman in a merchant company, arrives at Alexandria just as Arabi Pasha launches his nationalist revolt against European interference.

'It is quite possible that there will be trouble here before long,' Mr. Hoare remarked at dinner.

'I saw something in the paper about it,' Mr. Alston, the third mate, said; 'but I did not trouble to read through the accounts. What is it all about?'

'There has been a sort of peaceable revolution,' Mr. Hoare said.

'The colonels of the regiments in Cairo, headed by a general named Arabi Pasha, mutinied, and the viceroy had to give way to them.'

'What did they mutiny about?' the third mate asked.

'Well, in the first place they wanted privileges for the army, and in the second place they wanted a lot of Europeans who hold berths to be dismissed, and the government to be entirely in the hands of the natives. It is a sort of national movement, with the army at the head of it; and the viceroy, although still nominally the ruler of Egypt, is in fact little more than a cipher in the hands of Arabi and the colonels.'

Then comes a Victorian political judgement and justification for what is to come: 'They say the French are at the bottom of it, and it is likely enough. They have always been jealous of our influence in Egypt. However, I do not suppose we shall interfere in the matter, unless they break regularly out and ill-treat Europeans, and threaten to seize the canal or something of that sort.'

Jack and two other midshipmen are given the day off and go sight-seeing in Alexandria. After a description of children covered with flies—'I expect the coating of dirt is so thick that they do not feel it'—the midshipmen take a most British look at the other Europeans to be seen in Alexandria: 'What a rascally set the Europeans look! The Egyptians are gentlemen by the side of them. I fancy from what I have heard they are the sweepings of the European ports—Greeks, Italians, Maltese, and French. When a fellow makes it too hot at home for the place to hold him, he comes over here—'

The boys get caught in the riots and take shelter in the shop of two Italian brothers—the sweepings, no doubt, but useful on occasions. The rioters approach the shop. Henty was careful about God in his books; muscular Christianity was his line and during any crisis he permits a brief reference to the deity. The two Italians pray as they realize what may be coming: 'The two brothers knelt together before the figure of a saint in a little niche in the wall. The boys glanced at each other, and each, following the example of the Italians, knelt down by a chair and prayed for a minute or two. As they rose to their feet there was a sudden din below.'

The three midshipmen are captured by a Bey who keeps them hostage. While prisoners they are permitted to watch the bombardment of the city by the British fleet.

'It is downright awful, isn't it?' Arthur Hill said in a hushed voice. 'I've often thought I should like to see a sea-fight, but I never thought it would be as terrible as this.'

Henty, who had seen much of war, pays a handsome tribute to the Egyptians: 'The gallantry with which the Egyptian gunners stuck to their work was the object of surprise and admiration to the British sailors. It seemed scarce possible that men could work under so tremendous a fire as that to which they were exposed. The forts were literally torn to pieces, and at the end of the day were little better than heaps of ruins scattered thickly with the corpses of the Egyptian artillerymen.'

The boys escape, and after many adventures rejoin the English only to find that their ship has gone. They are therefore attached to Lord Charles Beresford who is engaged in that familiar imperial duty of restoring law and order. When an officer suggests it is bad news that Arabi Pasha has ordered all able-bodied men to join the army, another replies: 'I don't call the last part bad news. We shall have ten thousand men here in a short time, and the more of these scoundrels that are gathered together the better, so that we can end it at one blow. If Arabi does but stand there is no doubt as to the result. The thing that would puzzle us would be for him and his troops to march away into Upper Egypt and lead us a long dance there.'

The Dash for Khartoum is the second of the Egypt-Sudan trilogy;

it is also one of the best of all Henty's stories and will be treated separately in chapter eleven.

With Kitchener in the Soudan was published in 1903 after Henty's death and was written within a year or so of the events it describes. Its main characters—Kitchener and Wingate—were very much in the public eye at the time and, in his descriptive writing about the battle of Omdurman, Henty is again the war correspondent. Omdurman was of particular significance to Victorian England since it avenged the death of General Gordon. As Henty concludes his preface: 'Thus a land that had been turned into a desert by the terrible tyranny of the Mahdi and his successor was wrested from barbarism and restored to civilization, and the stain upon British honour caused by the desertion of Gordon by the British ministry of the day was wiped out. It was a marvellous campaign—marvellous in the perfection of its organization, marvellous in the completeness of its success.'

The hero's father is disinherited for marrying a clergyman's daughter—his father is the brother of an earl—and so the young couple go to Egypt since she is consumptive and needs a warm climate. The father only uses his first two names, dropping the family name of Hartley so as not to dishonour it, since he works as a clerk. He accompanies General Hicks on the ill-fated campaign of 1883 against the Mahdi and disappears. The mother brings the boy up in Egypt; he learns fluent Arabic as well as Soudanese and is imbued with the desire to find out what happened to his father. In due course he goes on Kitchener's campaign that brings about the defeat of the Mahdists and the reconquest of the Soudan.

There is a story within the story, for the hero, Gregory, finds his dead father's diary and discovers that he is the heir to the earldom as all those between him and the title have conveniently died. Gregory procures an introduction to Lord Cromer and then to Kitchener and so gets a place on the expedition. The imperial sentiments are clear; as Gregory sits on the steamer going up the Nile he muses: 'It was glorious to think that, in whatever humble capacity, he was yet one of the band who were on their way up to meet the hordes of the Khalifa, to rescue the Soudan from the tyranny under which it had groaned, to avenge Gordon and Hicks and the gallant men who had died with them!'

Gregory dives off his steamer into the Nile to rescue a woman who turns out to be the wife of one of the leading Mahdists, and

5

he is promptly captured. There follows a detailed description of the battle of Atbara. In due course Gregory escapes and returns to the British lines; he is reprimanded by Kitchener and reminded that an officer's life belongs to the service. Later Gregory is to tell someone: 'He [Kitchener] said there is a lot of good in these black fellows if one could but get at it. They have never had a chance yet, but, given good administration and the suppression of all tribal feuds with a stern hand, they might be moulded into anything.' Henty pays tribute to the brilliant organization which Kitchener maintained throughout his Nile expedition. Of the British soldier he says: 'The British soldier is ready to support any fatigue and any hardship with a prospect of a fight at the end, and during the advance he is always haunted by the fear that the enemy will retire or give in on his approach.'

A chapter is devoted to the battle of Omdurman. Henty compares the famous charge, in which twenty-two officers and men were killed and fifty wounded, to that of the 23rd Light Dragoons at Talavera: 'Both incidents were, like the Balaclava charge, magnificent, but they were not war.' He also repeatedly pays tribute to the bravery of the enemy soldiers, at one point making his hero reflect: 'And yet he could not but feel sorry for the valiant savages who under so awful a fire still pressed forward to certain death, their numbers withering away at every step until they dwindled to nothing, only to be replaced by a fresh band, which darted forward to meet a similar fate . . .' Total losses on the British side were 524 including the wounded.

The army enters Khartoum and Henty, ever ready with superlatives, says: 'The Mahdi's cause, the foulest and most bloodstained tyranny that had ever existed, transforming as it did a flourishing province into an almost uninhabited desert, was crushed for ever.' Later, he reminds his readers of Gordon and the feelings that the name aroused: 'The long-delayed duty which England owed to one of her noblest sons had been done: Gordon had had his burial.'

By Sheer Pluck takes us to West Africa. Henty accompanied the Wolseley expedition to the Gold Coast in 1873–1874 and his despatches were re-issued as *The March to Coomassie*. The hero of *By Sheer Pluck* goes on an expedition to the Gold Coast and ends up taking part in the war. Frank is taken on as his assistant by a naturalist, Mr. Goodenough. Before they leave England, Frank questions Mr. Goodenough as to whether he will hire men for their expedition in Sierra Leone. 'Certainly not, Frank. The negroes of Sierra Leone are the most indolent, the most worthless, and the most insolent in all Africa.' Thus disposing of the Sierra Leonians, Mr. Goodenough proceeds with a brief history lesson on the tribes of West Africa and their behaviour. Later, witnessing some native frolics, Mr. Goodenough expounds further:

'They are just like children. They are always either laughing or quarrelling. They are good-natured and passionate, indolent, but will work hard for a time; clever up to a certain point, densely stupid beyond. The intelligence of an average negro is about equal to that of a European child of ten years old . . . They are fluent talkers, but their ideas are borrowed. They are absolutely without originality, absolutely without inventive power. Living among white men, their imitative faculties enable them to attain a considerable amount of civilization. Left alone to their own devices they retrograde into a state little above their native savagery.'

Not surprisingly, a generation fed upon such Henty judgements would not only believe in its own superiority over most native peoples but also regard empire as legitimate, indeed a duty. The contempt in this book is sometimes glaring:

'Do you mean to say that there is a king in that wretched-looking village?' Frank asked in surprise.

'Kings are as plentiful as peas in Africa,' Mr. Goodenough said, 'but you will not see much royal state.'

There is of course a typical good native servant-assistant, Ostik, who knows his place and where his loyalty lies.

'You're not afraid, Ostik, because it is possible we may have trouble on the way?'

'Me not very much afraid, massa. You good massa to Ostik he no run away if fightee come; but no good fight whole tribe.'

'I hope not to have any fighting at all, Ostik; but as I have got six Houssas with me who will all carry breech-loading guns, I think we should be a match for a good-sized tribe, if necessary.' Ostik looked thoughtful. 'More easy, massa, go without Houssas,' he said. 'Black man not often touch white traveller.'

Despite this thoughtful advice, Mr. Goodenough takes his six
Houssas armed to the teeth and off they go into the interior. Ostik
speaks the kind of respectful pidgin expected of all natives. They
have various adventures which are liberally interspersed with useful
information about travelling in darkest Africa so that a boy could
end up with a tolerable knowledge of what to do when he himself
went empire-building. A typical description concerns porters
carrying white men in hammocks. After saying how they put turbans
in the shape of muffins on their heads and a board between two
men at the front and two at the rear, Henty goes on: 'They can trot
along at the rate of six miles an hour, for great distances, often
keeping up a monotonous song. Their action is perfectly smooth
and easy, and the traveller in the hammock, by shutting his eyes,
might imagine himself swinging in a cot on board ship on an almost
waveless sea.'

At one point, they come to a village where a 'civilized' headman
—an ex-slave from North America—lives. He gives them dinner:
'The dinner consisted of two fowls cut in half and grilled over a
fire, fried plantains, and, to the astonishment of the travellers, green
peas, followed by cold boiled rice over which honey had been
poured. Their host had placed plates only for two, but they would
not sit down until he had consented to join them.' Here is a nice
touch, typical of Henty, for though racial arrogance peeps through
most pages of this particular book there is also no hesitation in
showing this courtesy towards the old man who is, after all, their
host. He tells his story: as a youth he had been taken to America and
had many adventures before making a fortune and returning to his
native village where he was the rightful chief. The old man's tale
takes up a substantial portion of the centre of the book and at one
point he discourses upon slavery. He tells how he was sold by one
master to another:

'Dat de curse of slabery, sar. Me trabel a good deal, and me tink
dat no working people in de world are so merry and happy as de
slabe in a plantation wid a good massa and missy. Dey not work
so hard as de white man. Dey have plenty to eat and drink, dey
hab deir gardens and deir fowls. When dey are sick dey are taken
care ob, when dey are ole they are looked after and hab noting to
do. I have heard people talk a lot of nonsense about de hard life
of de plantation slabe. Dat not true, sar, wid a good massa. De

slabe hab no care and he bery happy. If all massas were good, and dere were a law dat if a plantation were broken up de slabes must be sold in families together, me tell you dat de life on a plantation a thousand times happier dan de life ob a black man in his own country.'

This is an apologia for slavery (comparable to a similar defence in *With Lee in Virginia*) which the enemies of Wilberforce could hardly have bettered.

In Dahomey they come up against warlike amazons and Frank— the true young gentleman—is appalled at the possibility that they may have to fight women:

'But it will seem dreadful to fire at women!' Frank said.

'That is merely an idea of civilization, Frank,' returns Mr. Goodenough.

He proceeds to lecture Frank upon different attitudes towards women in Europe where a man is 'considered a brute and a coward who lifts his hand against a woman. Among the lower classes wife and woman beating is by no means uncommon;' and so, somewhat casuistically, he leads Frank to understand that women may be killed in Africa. Frank is still not convinced: 'Still, I sha'n't like having to fire at women.'

After the death of Mr. Goodenough the story moves rapidly into the Ashanti War. Explaining the background to this Henty says: 'About this time Mr. Hennessey, whose repeated blunders had in no slight degree contributed to the invasion, was relieved by Mr. Keate, who at once wholly alienated the Fantis by telling them that they must defend themselves, as the English had nothing more to do with the affair than to defend their forts. Considering that the English had taken the natives under their protection, and that the war was caused entirely by the taking over of Elmina by the English and by their breach of faith to the natives there, this treatment of the Fantis was as unjust as it was impolitic.' Henty favoured a forward policy—but an honourable forward policy. In his many diversions of this nature he never writes down to his juvenile audience: his style is clear and easy to understand yet adult for all that.

Henty certainly shared the prevalent belief in the laziness of Africans and, in passages such as the following, he must have done a good deal to assist the growth of the worst kind of image peddled eighty or ninety years later by white settlers in Kenya and the Rhodesias as they fought their own rearguard actions: 'The natives of Africa are capable of great exertion for a time, but their habitual attitude is that of extreme laziness. One week's work in the year suffices to plant a sufficient amount of ground to supply the wants of a family. The seed only requires casting into the earth, and soon the ground will be covered with melons and pumpkins. Sweet potatoes and yams demand no greater cultivation, and the bananas and plantains require simply to be cut. For fifty-one weeks in the year the negro simply sits down and watches his crops grow. To people like these time is of absolutely no value. Their wants are few . . .'

Henty mixes these attitudes with his development of Frank as the ideal paternalist white among blacks. Frank is taken prisoner by the Ashantis. He has large supplies of the medicines Mr. Goodenough had brought and uses them to cure sick Africans. The chief, his captor, says: 'I wish I could let you go. You are a good white man, and my soldiers love you for the pains you take going amongst them when they are sick, and giving them the medicine of the whites. But I dare not do it. As you know when the king is wroth the greatest tremble . . .'

The Ashanti War proceeds and the natives lose. Describing their tactics, Henty is disingenuous: 'But it is characteristic of all savages that they can never be got to rush down upon a foe who is prepared and well armed. A half dozen white men have been known to keep a whole tribe of Red Indians at a distance on the prairie. This, however, can be accounted for by the fact that the power of the chiefs is limited, and that each Indian values his own life highly and does not care to throw it away on a desperate enterprise. Among the Ashantis, however, where the power of the chiefs is very great and where life is held of little account, it is singular that such tactics should not have been adopted.' Henty provides the answer to his own problem here, but credits the Africans neither with the sense not to throw their lives away nor with possessing an estimate of their own value.

Henty describes how all the able-bodied men in Cape Coast are rounded up to act as porters for Wolseley's advance into the interior. Assuming, with colonial administrators for a long time to come, that the Africans should want to serve their new white masters, for whatever purpose, Henty says of these conscripted porters: 'The indignation of some of the men thus seized, loaded, and sent up country under a strong escort was very funny, and their astonishment in some cases altogether unfeigned.' And so he adds his quota to another of the myths: the funny native. And yet after a battle Henty can say: 'They fought with extraordinary pluck and resolution, as was shown by the fact that although wretchedly armed, for upwards of five hours they resisted the attack of troops armed with breech loaders, and supported by guns and rockets.'

The last campaign in *Through Three Campaigns* is set in West Africa: the Ashanti War of 1900–1901. Its hero, Bullen, is insufferable. On the subject of endurance, reflecting the then ascendant imperial-racial view, he says: 'I should hate to be beaten by a native.' There are endless details of the campaign; there is little story. Bullen, in a few short years, has become the archetypal white in a colonial environment:

'But here is the boy with our supper, which we have fairly earned, and to which I shall certainly do justice. What have you got, boy?'
'Half a tin of preserved meat, sah, done up with curry.'
'Let us eat with thankfulness. How much more curry have we got, boy?'
'Three bottles, sah.'

Towards the end of the story Bullen and another officer, Hallett, are lost in the forest. They come to a huge armed camp of the enemy and walk boldly in and persuade them to surrender (an episode designed to show the fearlessness, initiative and sheer impact of the white man) although admitting that they themselves are lost. They each earn the D.S.O. for this. When the chiefs promise to accompany Bullen and Hallett back to Coomassie to negotiate a surrender Bullen talks to them just like any district officer: 'We respect brave men, and are anxious that there should be an end to this fighting. When it is over, you will again live under the protection of our government, and the past will be forgotten . . .' By this time in the story Bullen is all of twenty-one. Understandably, perhaps, a fourteen-year-old reading this would believe that most things were possible for the white man in Africa.

Henty's other African books concern South Africa. Before he was either an imperialist or a racist Henty was a nationalist, and this comes across clearly in his preface to *The Young Colonists* ('A Tale of the Zulu and Boer Wars'): 'After having written upwards of fifty records of almost unbroken success to the British arms in almost all parts of the world, I have found it painful to describe these two campaigns in which we suffered defeat. I trust, however, that this story will prove of great interest to the reader because of the characteristic English pluck and daring of its hero.' The book contains its quota of paternalist statements such as 'two or three white men together can do anything with the natives . . .' Mr. Harvey, one of the main characters in the story, is a good paternalist but not prepared for any nonsense:

> 'Steady!' Mr. Harvey shouted; 'push on ahead; but each man keep to his work—the first who attempts to run and desert the waggons I will shoot through the head.'

The book includes a brief account of the Anglo-Boer War of 1881–1882. The battles of Laing's Nek and Majuba are described and when, at the end of the war, the British concede what the Boers want Henty makes a point that liberals were to repeat in the century that followed: 'Not only were the natives practically abandoned to the mercy of the Boers, to be shot down or enslaved at their will, as in former times, but . . .'

Henty wrote *With Buller in Natal* ('A Born Leader')—the subtitle refers to Chris, the young hero—while the Boer War was still being fought. As he claims in his preface, 'I have, however, endeavoured to reconcile the various narratives of the fighting in Natal, and to make the account of the military occurrences as clear as possible. Fortunately this is not a history, but a story, to which the war forms the background . . .'

The hero, Chris, is somewhat machine-like: with twenty other youngsters, all the sons of gentlemen, mainly from Johannesburg mining families, they form an independent scouting unit that is attached to the army but on condition they can resign whenever they want. One important factor in this story is that Henty writes as a war correspondent and, though deeply critical of Buller and the conduct of the campaign, his criticisms are tempered by an obvious desire not to say anything that may be construed as unpatriotic while the war is actually in progress. It is a difficult combination for him to manage and he is not entirely successful.

The other aspect which has immense interest, in view of developments in South Africa during the 1960s and 1970s, is the British opinion of the Boers which Henty presents. Early on, speaking of the position of the Uitlanders in the Transvaal, he says. 'Never before had a large body of intelligent men been kept in a state of abject subjection by an inferior race, a race almost without even the elements of civilization, ignorant and brutal beyond any existing white community, and superior only in the fact that they were organized and armed, whereas those they trampled upon were deficient in both these respects.' Later he adds: 'The Boer government was corrupt from the highest to the lowest.' And, looking forward to anti-apartheid arguments of a later age, Chris's father explains to him when the war is about to break out that he will stay in Johannesburg and work the mines: 'For myself, I would risk any loss or damage rather than aid in supplying them with gold, but for the sake of our shareholders in Europe I must do my best to save the mines from destruction.'

There was war hysteria in Britain at the time and Henty excels himself in his denigration of the Boers: 'They were indeed as unsavoury in appearance as they were brutal in manner. Water is scarce in the Transvaal, and is used most sparingly for all purposes of cleanliness. The Boer sleeps in his clothes, gives himself a shake when he gets up, and his toilet is completed, unless on very exceptional occasions, when he goes outside the door to the water cask, fills his hands with water, and rubs them over his face.' Later he says: 'In dress the Boer is almost universally slovenly, his clothes hang about him stained and discoloured by long usage. In the majority of cases he is altogether without education, and very many Boers are scarcely able to sign their names.'

Chris soon establishes himself as the leader of his volunteer group. On one occasion he knocks down a beastly Boer farmer who has refused to provide water for the women and children in a party trekking to the British lines:

'Now you can get up, you hulking ruffian. I am going to give you a lesson in civility. Oh, you won't get up! Well, it will make no difference to me;' and he proceeded to give the howling Boer a tremendous thrashing.

Towards the end of the story when the boys discuss their achievements they express satisfaction at the number of Boers they have killed while none of them has been killed. Chris thoughtfully adds: 'I should be sorry even to lose one of our blacks.' Henty often refers to the treachery of the Boers: 'But here, as upon almost every occasion, the enemy paid no respect whatever to the Geneva emblem, although when, as once or twice happened, one of our shells fell near an ambulance of theirs, they had sent in indignant protests against our conduct.'

Victorian public school morality is introduced near the end by the insufferable Chris when one of his stout chaps, Carmichael, complains, very mildly, that they have been going at one hell of a pace:

'No doubt you have,' Chris said, 'a thundering good day's work; but a fellow is not worth calling a fellow if he can't manage to do two days' work at a stretch for once in a way.'

With Roberts to Pretoria is one of the last books Henty wrote; it is an example of his matured boys' story style and is important as a key to many of his attitudes. The young hero, Yorke, goes out to South Africa to stay with a cousin since his clergyman father has suddenly lost his private income and the family is in reduced circumstances. Yorke is welcomed at his cousin's farm although the latter is married to a Dutch woman whose sympathies are with the Boers. Trouble is coming but for a few months Yorke learns Dutch and with practice becomes a first-class rifleshot. He also makes an enemy of a young Dutchman, Dirck Jansen, who reappears a number of times in the story, tries to murder Yorke and is finally killed. Yorke enlists as a scout when the war begins and has adventures behind the enemy lines: he is accompanied by a faithful Dutch lad, Hans, and by Peter, a devoted Kaffir follower. He takes part in the Methuen campaigns and then gets on to the staff of General Roberts as he advances to Pretoria.

What is especially fascinating about this book is its reflection of a number of High Victorian attitudes: to class, race and empire.

Early in the story Mr. Allnutt, Yorke's cousin, describes his wife's opinions, and there is a contemporary ring to what he has to say: 'There is an association called the Africander Bond, and its object, as far as I can see, is to establish the supremacy of the Dutch in Africa.' Later when he tells how he has built up his farm he says: 'It took a lot of work, but Kaffir labour is cheap.' When Kruger's ultimatum sparks off the war, Yorke is told: 'This ultimatum is a glorious thing. No one can say that we forced the war upon them. It puts a stop to all these negotiations and settles the question. It has got to be fought out now; and, thank God, we have not got a government that will permit another Majuba surrender. I expect we shall have hard fighting for a time.'

The importance Henty attached to public schools is emphasized a number of times. When Yorke is given a commission and thanks the major in the local volunteer corps in which he is to serve, the major replies: 'I had the more pleasure in granting the colonel's request, inasmuch as I am myself a public-school boy. I am an Etonian, and can quite understand your eagerness to take part in the business.' Yorke meets Cecil Rhodes: 'Yorke looked with interest at the man who is the Napoleon of South Africa . . .' Rhodes asks the hero for an account of his adventures. On the make in an unashamed Victorian way:

> Yorke felt that in this strong able man he might find a valuable friend, therefore he gave him a sketch of his reasons for leaving England.
>
> 'So you were at Rugby!' his hearer broke in. 'I am a public-school boy myself, you know, and there is always a fellow-feeling among public-school boys, even if they were not at the same school.'

The hero's Kaffir follower, Peter, is an excellent example of a loyal, simple native ready to be instructed by his master. Yorke obliges. Peter admits a liking for liquor and says, that though it is against the law for natives, there are always men ready to sell it to them for good money.

> 'They are bad men, Peter. The harm they do is very great. That is why so many of your people are in rags, though they can earn pay when they are willing to work. They will only labour for three or four days, and then spend pretty well all they have earned on spirits, and be drunk the next three.'
>
> 'That is true, baas. Peter do that very often. Big fool, Peter! Often tells himself so when he gets sober. But when he gets money he smells spirit, then he makes fool of himself again.'
>
> 'Well, you had better make up your mind to give it up al-together, Peter. You are getting good pay now, and ought to have a lot of money saved by the end of the war—enough to go back to your own people and build a kraal, and buy cattle, and exchange some of them for a wife.'
>
> 'That true, baas. Peter will try not to be big fool again.'

In an interesting chapter upon the battle of Magersfontein, Henty appears singularly not to connect cause and effect. He is fair in describing the British defeat. The attack has been launched silently in the dark by the British against the Boer position on a kopje and, as Henty admits, 'It is certain, however, that had the usual precautions been adopted (no scouts were sent out in advance) the catastrophe that followed would have been avoided.' The British suffer very heavy losses and at one point some soldiers break and flee back to their camp. Henty defends them: 'For once nature had overcome the dauntless spirit of some of the finest soldiers in the world. For thirteen hours they had been under tremendous fire; during that time they had been practically without orders . . . Their inability to do aught but suffer had broken them down. It speaks highly indeed for the discipline and courage of these soldiers that at Paardeberg they should have entirely recovered their morale, and have shown their old conspicuous bravery, unsurpassed by that of any other regiment.' Yet before the battle, which was a disaster, Henty says: 'All in the camp were filled with excitement. It was certain that the time was at hand when they would meet the foe in strength face to face, and, formidable as was the position, no one doubted the result.' At no time does Henty make any connexion between British attitudes of arrogant superiority, which he depicts freely enough, and their failure to judge the enemy correctly.

Victorian money consciousness is clearly brought out when Mr. Chambers, a mining magnate who has befriended Yorke, offers him a future at the end of the war. In reply to a question about his meeting with Rhodes, Yorke says: 'He asked me if I intended to stop in the army after the war is over. I said that I had no idea of doing so, as I had come out with the intention of making money. He was good enough to speak flatteringly of my having learned to speak Dutch so soon, and said that if, when things were settled, I would go to him, he would find a berth for me and push me forward.' Mr. Chambers, however, is determined to push Yorke forward and so, as he lies in bed that night, Yorke can reminisce: 'I do think I am the luckiest fellow going . . . In the first place, I get a commission in the army; in the second, I obtain Mr. Rhodes's good-will; and now Mr. Chambers, one of the richest men in Johannesburg, is going to take me up, and all from a series of accidents . . .' (That, indeed, is the pattern for most Henty heroes.) Henty gives sketches of both Roberts and Kitchener. Of the latter he says: 'With every faculty concentrated upon his work Lord Kitchener never spared himself, and he expected an equal devotion to duty from all under his command, officers and men alike. He was a man of iron, one who could make but small allowance for the weakness of others, would admit of no carelessness, and had no sympathy with the love of amusement and the easy-going manner of doing work that were characteristic of no inconsiderable proportion of the younger officers of the army . . . He was admired and respected, but he had not Lord Roberts's knack of making himself loved by all with whom he came in contact.'

The war over, Yorke resigns his commission and goes to work for Mr. Chambers and learn mining. Hans, his Dutch follower, stays on as his servant and to mind the stables. Yorke asks Peter whether he wants to go back to his tribe but the faithful Kaffir replies: 'I shall not do that, baas, as long as you will keep me. Some day I will go down and buy a wife, and build a little house near here. I have been so long in towns that I do not want to be a wild fellow again, and live in village kraals, and eat mealies, and have nothing to do but walk about and carry a gun on my shoulder. A stupid life that; much rather live with baas.' So Yorke settles in South Africa.

More even than the Indian books, Henty's African stories highlight his attitudes to race, to empire and to his general concept of white—and British—superiority.

CHAPTER TEN

The American Stories

HENTY'S BOOKS ENJOYED enormous popularity in North America both during his lifetime and long afterwards, although the huge and cut-throat American pirating industry must have deprived him of most of the profits from his transatlantic sales. He wrote six full-length stories about the continent, one of them about Canada. *With Wolfe in Canada*, as the name implies, is a straightforward history; its period is contemporaneous with another story, *True to the Old Flag*, about the American War of Independence, in which Henty sets out to put the historical record straight.

More interesting, however, are his four books about the United States in the nineteenth century: *Captain Bayley's Heir*, *With Lee in Virginia*, *Redskin and Cowboy* and *In the Heart of the Rockies*. *With Lee in Virginia* is about the Civil War, but the other three may be described as early westerns. Henty also wrote one short story about the West—'White Faced Dick'— and a long short story, 'In the Hands of the Cave Dwellers', which is set in Mexico and deals with adventures among the Apaches and other Indians.

Henty's preface to *With Wolfe in Canada* begins: 'In the present volume I have endeavoured to give the details of the principal events in a struggle whose importance can hardly be overrated.' His point is the mastery of North America, yet Henty at once has to make a concession: 'It is true that in time the North American colonies, with the exception of Canada, broke away . . .' In fact they did so almost as soon as the Canadian question had been settled and, though France thereafter took second place to Britain as an imperial power, British mastery of the North American continent was indeed to be short-lived.

There is a long prelude set in England before the hero, James Walsham, arrives in Canada. Then chapter nine, 'The Defeat of Braddock', takes us into the war for Canada. There is an interesting historical observation made by Henty about French and English attitudes:

> There can be no doubt that had they been able to look into the future every Indian on the continent would have joined the French in their effort to crush the English colonies. Had France remained master of America the Indians might even now be roaming free and unmolested on the lands of their forefathers. France is not a colonizing nation; she would have traded with the Indians, would have endeavoured to Christianize them, and would have left them their land and freedom well satisfied with the fact that the flag of France should wave over so vast an extent of country; but on England conquering the soil, her armies of emigrants pressed west, and the red man is fast becoming extinct on the continent of which he was once the lord.

Of the colonial armies voted by the assemblies to fight in Canada, Henty says: 'In point of morals the army, composed almost entirely of farmers and farmers' sons, was exemplary. It is recorded that not a chicken was stolen.'

Henty's junction technique is used in all his historical novels. First there is a history lesson to set the scene—here, for example, a description of Montcalm's career and his arrival in Canada: ' . . . Montcalm learned that the expedition which had just left New York was destined for Louisburg, he was at liberty to utilize his army for the invasion of the defenceless colonies, and he determined to commence the campaign by the capture of Fort William Henry.' Then, when all is set for the military action, along comes the hero: 'James Walsham with his company of Royal Scouts had spent the spring at Fort William Henry.'

Nat, the scout, instructs James how to elude Indians at night. It is a Henty trick, during his instructional passage, first to make the reader realize what foolish mistakes others (those who lose battles, for example) have made but then to encourage his young readers to imagine that, in the right circumstances, they could themselves be more successful.

Henty has some tart comments on military incompetents; of General Webb he says: 'But as he was neither brave nor determined, he remained at Fort Edward sending off message after message to New York for help which could not possibly arrive in time.' Henty makes the capture of Quebec an exciting episode; he then adds his historical footnote: 'In point of numbers engaged and in the total loss on both sides the fight on the Plains of Abraham does not deserve to rank as a great battle, but its results were of the most extreme importance, for the victory transferred Canada from France to England.'

With Wolfe in Canada (apart from the hero's adventures in England at the beginning) is basically an historical treatment of the English defeat of the French. In *True to the Old Flag*, however, there occur some more debatable Henty historical judgements. He starts his preface:

> You have probably been accustomed to regard the war between England and her Colonies in America as one in which we were not only beaten but to some extent humiliated. Owing to the war having been an unsuccessful one for our arms, British writers have avoided the subject, and it has been left for American historians to describe. These, writing for their own countrymen, and drawing for their facts upon gazettes, letters, and other documents emanating from one side only, have naturally, and no doubt insensibly, given a very strong colour to their own views of the events, and English writers have been too much inclined to accept their account implicitly. There is, however, another and very different side to the story, and this I have endeavoured to show you. The whole of the facts and details connected with the war, can be relied upon as accurate.
>
> . . . You will see that although unsuccessful—and success was, under the circumstances, a sheer impossibility—the British troops fought with a bravery which was never exceeded, and that their victories in actual conflict vastly outnumbered their defeats. Indeed it may be doubted whether in any war in which this country has been engaged have our soldiers exhibited the qualities of endurance and courage in a higher degree.

At the beginning of the story the young hero, Harold Wilson, is sent from Massachusetts by his father to stay with cousins on the frontier by Lake Huron. There the boy learns Indian fighting and woodcraft. Henty's American dialogue almost foreshadows Zane Grey. Harold is back with his father, Captain Wilson, when a deputation arrives to persuade him to join the rebels. Wilson refuses and the deputation departs. Harold asks his father to explain 'the exact position in which matters stood' and there follow historical explanations of the colonies' grievances, the Stamp Act and the mutual incomprehension which has produced the war. The language is straightforward and the explanations impartial. Thus a paragraph begins: 'In England neither the spirit nor the strength of the colonists was understood.' It was this simplicity in delivering history lessons in the middle of his stories that made Henty's books such favourites as school prizes for a generation.

The battle of Lexington follows and the war is underway. There are numerous historical explanations. A typical paragraph starts. 'Men like Washington, and Franklin, and Adams may have desired only that the colonists should be free from imperial taxation, but the popular voice went far beyond this.' Henty, generally, is impartial, yet in this book he makes clear his determination to redress the wrong impressions about the war which, he contends, then existed: 'The efforts of American writers, however, to conceal the real facts of the case, to minimize the rebellious language, the violent acts of the colonists, and to make England responsible for the war because a body of troops were sent to seize cannon (the spark that led to Lexington) and military stores intended to be used against them, are so absurd, as well as so untrue, that it is astonishing how wide a credence such statements have received.'

Bunker's Hill rates a chapter and of the first quarter of the book a good third is history. Then Harold's father allows him to become a scout with a frontiersman, Peter Lambton, as part of an irregular force. He is accompanied by a faithful negro servant, Jake, who is to remain with him to the end of the story. At first Lambton, the leader of the scouting party, is furious with Jake whose 'habit of bursting into fits of laughter on the smallest provocation, as is the manner of his race, enraged the scout to the last degree'. This is one of many Henty stereotype negroes.

Henty is unsparing in his criticisms of the English generals. Of Howe he says: 'His supineness during the past four months had virtually lost the American colonies to England.' After describing Howe's abandoning Boston, Henty continues: 'Howe's conduct in this was on a piece with his behaviour throughout the campaign; he was, however, little if at all inferior to the other generals, who vied with each other in incapacity and folly. Never, indeed, in the whole history of England were her troops led by men so inefficient, so sluggish, and so incapable as those who commanded her armies in the American revolutionary war.' Such a passage is reminiscent of Henty the war correspondent.

Peter the scout and Harold come upon a neutral farmer and, posing as a revolting colonist, Peter counters the farmer's cautious suggestion that so far the English have been winning. There is some Henty mockery of boastful Americans in the following passage:

> 'That is so,' Peter agreed. 'But every one knows that the Americans are just the bravest people on the face of the habitable earth. I reckon that their dander is not fairly up yet; but when they begin in earnest you will see what they will do.'

Interspersed between the main events of the war come Harold's scouting adventures, although this was plainly a history book first and foremost. When his father decides to return to England, Harold goes again to Canada to serve as a scout under Burgoyne whose exploits are then described. The last major adventure of Harold and his friends comes when they set off to rescue two girls who have been carried off by Indians. There is little activity on the war front, winter is setting in and they have to travel far into the territory of the Iroquois Indians. Harold, his faithful Jake and the scouts duly rescue the girls but are then trapped on an island in a lake which has frozen. Henty provides an astonishingly vivid description of a terrible storm which leads to the break-up of the ice.

Back in the war, Harold is briefly captured but Jake rescues him; thereafter the book is mainly concerned with the history of the war up to its conclusion. 'Loyalists' a hundred years later would have found it excellent teaching material.

Captain Bayley's Heir ('A Tale of the Goldfields of California'), is not a history. It is one of Henty's best yarns: partly about boys at Westminster school and some villainy between two cousins; and partly about the United States where the hero goes when in disgrace. He works on a river boat on the Mississippi, crosses the continent with a waggon train of emigrants and then works in the California gold rush.

Frank Norris is wrongfully accused of stealing money at school and his cousin, clearly the villain of the piece, who had planted the money, encourages him to flee—which he foolishly does. The reason for this villainy is that only one can be Captain Bayley's heir; in fact the real heir (son of the Captain's runaway daughter) turns out to be a crippled boy who had been brought up by a working-class family—a bit of Henty high sentiment.

Frank gets a passage on a ship to America and in New Orleans obtains a temporary job on a Mississippi cargo sailing barge. The Americans in the south all talk of 'niggers'. There are excellent descriptions of the Mississippi River and the work on it. In a terrible storm the boat is stranded, enmeshed in a tree, and the negro crew for a while is trapped: 'Do you hear them niggers holloaing like so many tom-cats? What good do they suppose that will do?' Later when the negroes are freed Hiram who runs the boat says to Frank:

'Still, one can't expect men of one colour to have the same ways as those of another, and I am bound to say that if the boat had gone down your boss would have lost four good pieces of property. Feel more comfortable—eh?'

The negroes grinned assent. Easily cast down, their spirits were as easily raised, and seeing that the white men appeared to consider that there was no urgent danger, they soon plucked up their courage.

Frank suggests they offer up a prayer for their safety; Hiram agrees though not normally a praying man. This is one of the comparatively rare Henty references to God. Later, as the negroes sing, Hiram says: 'Just like children, ain't they?'

They fight river pirates and then Frank goes to Omaha and joins a waggon train. There is a good description of the monotony, the day-to-day problems, the hunters getting meat, hauling the waggons through difficult places, the buffalo herds and the prairie wild life. Henty indeed is a fund of information for future writers of cowboy stories. Abe the hunter describes the Red Indians: 'Now, you know, the redskins ain't to be despised. You may hate them, you may say they are a cussed lot of rascals and thieves, but there ain't no despising them, and any one as does that is sure to have cause to repent it, sooner or later.'

The waggon train is attacked by a large Indian party but successfully fights them off. The journey to California takes five months; then the five hunters of whom Frank by now has become a member leave to search for gold.

The diggers make money but no great fortune; Frank befriends a young man with a sick father and these two subsequently strike it rich. The father had been a solicitor and taken to drink but now, thanks to Frank, can return home and redeem himself. He spends months searching for Captain Bayley and his niece, Alice, who are on tour in Europe, in order to tell Alice that Frank maintains his innocence. When he hears this, Captain Bayley, Harry (his newly found heir) and Alice set out for California.

Frank has become a hero in his part of California where he saves a coach from robbers. There are good descriptions of the gold-digging camps. When Captain Bayley discovers Frank they work out how the cousin managed to frame him. They go to Sacramento where Captain Bayley has left Alice—the gold camps were not the place for a young lady—and Frank finds she is now a beautiful eighteen-year-old.

> 'There, that's enough, Frank,' she said presently. 'You mustn't do that any more, you know, because I am grown up, and you know we are not really even cousins.'
>
> 'Cousins or not, Alice,' Frank said, laughing, 'I have kissed you from the time you were a child, and if you suppose I am going to give it up now, when there is a real pleasure in kissing you, you are mistaken, I can tell you.'

This is about the nearest Henty ever comes to a 'sexy' passage in any of his boys' books.

They return home to England; Fred, the villain, is exposed though not publicly; Frank is exonerated at his beloved Westminster school and all is set for a happy ending.

Things do not go well with Fred: 'After some years of useless attempts to make his way, he was glad to accept the offer of a petty judgeship in India, and there, ten years later, he died, stabbed to the heart by a Mahomedan dacoit whom he had sentenced to a term of imprisonment.' Frank ends up in Parliament where, 'he can always be depended upon to vote with his party, and he occasionally makes vigorous and indignant attacks against any policy which he believes to be lowering the *prestige* and position of his country'.

With Lee in Virginia is a fine romantic novel about a young southern gentleman rather than a history. Henty's sympathies are clearly with the south and the hero is heir to a great estate in Virginia. His father is of English origin and Vincent Wingfield— sixteen at the start—has been educated in England. At the commencement of the story he is telling the overseer not to whip a slave. Henty in this as in other stories (for instance *By Sheer Pluck*) is ambivalent about slavery which he tries, if not to justify, at least to excuse. He does so by attempting to show that most owners were good to their slaves, who were indeed better off in that condition than if they had been free. At the same time he feels obliged to condemn the institution of slavery which he does half-heartedly by saying that bad masters abuse it.

In this preface Henty promises to confine the history to the central part of the struggle (how the northern armies tried to force their way to Richmond, the heart of the confederacy), and adds: 'Even in recounting the leading events in these campaigns, I have burdened my story with as few details as possible, it being my object now, as always, to amuse as well as to give instruction in the facts of history.'

The opening of the story is devoted to slavery; in England Vincent has absorbed much of the feeling against it and his father early on gives him a lecture to show that there are good and bad masters and that more are good than bad: 'I consider that the slave with a fairly kind master is to the full as happy as the ordinary English labourer . . . They will still have to work for their living as they do now, [if freed] and being naturally indolent and shiftless would probably fare much worse . . . Therefore, Vincent, my advice to you is, be always kind to your slaves—not over-indulgent, because they are very like children and indulgence spoils them . . .'

Vincent breaks in a horse called Wildfire; there is an evil overseer; Mr. Lincoln is elected President. Vincent interferes to stop a neighbour, Jackson, a small landowner 'upstart', from flogging a slave. In revenge Jackson sells the slave's 'wife' and child but Vincent hears of this and gets his lawyer to buy the woman and child for him. Tom, the slave, runs away and Vincent provides him with a passage to England. Thus, Henty has things all ways: he is on the side of the romantic south; he makes his hero a knight-errant who helps good slaves against cruel masters; he does not upset the system.

Then comes the war and, amid southern enthusiasm, young Vincent joins a cavalry troop under a Major Ashley. (One may speculate, since so many of the ingredients are present in this book, whether Margaret Mitchell chanced upon it before she wrote *Gone with the Wind*.) Vincent is soon commissioned. Stonewall Jackson (not to be confused with the 'upstart') features quite prominently in the story and Henty tells the incident that produced his nickname. There is a description of the *Merrimac*, a sort of early impromptu 'ironclad', the sinking of the *Cumberland* and *Congress* and then the battle between the *Monitor* and *Merrimac*.

On one of his cavalry exploits Vincent is captured and finds the horrible Jackson a prisoner too. His faithful servant-slave, Dan, helps him escape. Foolishly he lets Jackson come with him and then they part. On the run—he is only eighteen but disguised as a minister of the church—Vincent thrashes a bully on a train. Then he reads that his disguise is known to the Federals and realizes that Jackson has betrayed him.

He comes to a small isolated house where a girl befriends him: 'The girl paid no attention to her words [of her old nurse], but stood waiting Vincent's answer. He did not hesitate. There was something in her face that told him, friend or foe, she was not likely to betray a fugitive . . .' Bushwackers (led by the man Vincent had thrashed on the train) come to seize Vincent but Lucy refuses to betray him. Vincent and Dan rescue Lucy and, with the old nurse, the four of them set off to reach the Confederate lines. They get round to calling each other by their first names, he Vin, she Lucy. Vincent has been wounded in the fight with the bushwackers and they hide up in a deserted farm house. Lucy fetches a doctor and, as he returns with her, he says 'with a rather slight twinkle of his eye': 'My patient must be quite an interesting fellow, young lady. A very knight-errant.'

Once Vincent is better they set off to pass through the lines to the south and thence to Antioch, in Georgia, where Lucy normally lives with two aunts. At the end of their journey Vincent asks Lucy whether she is sorry it is over. She hesitates with quivering lip and then says it is always a pity to say goodbye. Vincent hopes it is not for long.

'I shall be back here as soon as this horrible war is over.'

'What for?' the girl asked, looking round in surprise. 'You live a long way from here, and you told me you knew nobody in these parts.'

'I know you.' Vincent said, 'and that is quite enough. Do you not know that I love you?'

The girl gave a start of surprise, her cheek flushed, but her eyes did not drop as she looked frankly at him.

'No, Vin,' she said after a pause, 'I never once thought you loved me, never once. You have not been a bit like what I thought people were when they felt like that.'

'I hope not, Lucy. I was your protector . . .'

As a southern gentleman he has, of course, behaved correctly (one might add as a Henty hero too). Then the girl admits she loves him with all her heart. After these avowals, Vincent says: 'It is horrid to have to sit here in this stiff, unnatural way, Lucy, when one is inclined to do something outrageous from sheer happiness.' He obviously wants to kiss her.

They reach Lucy's aunts.

'And who is this officer, Lucy?' Miss Kingston asked rather anxiously.

'He is a Virginian gentleman, auntie. His mother has large estates near Richmond . . .'

She assures her aunts that Vincent has behaved just like a brother—as Jack would have done. 'That's right, my dear; I am glad to hear it. Now, let us hear all about it.'

When Vincent comes to the house—he has let Lucy meet her aunts on her own—they send him into a room to wait for Lucy. 'Lucy required several calls before she came down. A new shyness such as she had never before felt had seized her, and it was with flushed cheeks and timid steps that she at last came downstairs, and it needed an encouraging—"Go in, you silly child, your lover will not eat you," before she turned the handle and went into the room where Vincent was expecting her.'

Vincent returns home to tell his mother and two sisters he is engaged; his mother's brow clears when she realizes that the engagement is to a southern girl and not some yankee woman who might have helped her son escape. Though grieved, his mother expects Vincent to be off to the front again at once. Meanwhile, however, Dinah the slave girl and her child have been abducted and Jonas Pearson the overseer has been dismissed by Mrs. Wingfield for falsifying the accounts. Vincent turns detective and tracks down Pearson who, in collaboration with Jackson's father, has abducted Dinah. Pearson turns out to be a notorious wanted man from thirteen years earlier. There is a shoot-out at the edge of the swamps, Pearson is killed—so is the sheriff—and Dinah is rescued.

By then the war is going badly for the south. Vincent volunteers to spy behind the enemy lines but is spotted by Jackson who is now a turncoat in the Federal army. Vincent kills him but is arrested. Waiting to be shot at dawn, Vincent is rescued by the faithful Tony (whom he helped to escape to England at the beginning of the book and who now turns up in one of the Negro battalions). There is an essential Henty passage about lying: 'Vincent considered that while in disguise, and doing important service for his country, he was justified in using deceit; but merely for the purpose of saving his own life, and that perhaps uselessly, he would not lie.'

Back from these adventures, Vincent counsels his mother to free the slaves at once, provide each with a plot on the estate, pay them for work so as to forestall the otherwise inevitable desertion which would follow the end of the war, and instead keep them loyal. This sage advice works. At the end of the book Henty says: 'More liberal terms were never granted by a conqueror to the vanquished'; and 'For a majority of the freed slaves very soon discovered that their lot was a far harder one than it had been before, and that freedom so suddenly given was a curse rather than a blessing to them.'

The really fascinating aspect of *Redskin and Cowboy* is that Henty managed to write a first-class western a generation before Zane Grey and a whole subsequent family of writers began to tackle the subject. And clearly he got it right. The book has all the ingredients of a modern western: the young hero is nicknamed 'Lightning' because of his fast draw; there are fights with Indians, a waggon train journey, a cattle round-up and a cattle drive, bad men, brigands, Mexicans and a gold camp.

In his preface Henty says: 'The picture I have given of their life [the cowboys] can be relied upon . . .' and the claim is fair. Not unlike Dickens, whose picture of the United States was not especially beloved of Americans, Henty gives some amusing glimpses of life at the time. Here, for instance, is a meal in a Texas hotel: 'Scarcely a word was spoken during the meal. It was evidently considered a serious business, and the chief duty of each man was to eat as much as possible in the shortest possible time.'

The descriptions, though couched in more antiquated language, are much the same as those appearing in later westerns:

> 'They look pretty hard,' Bill Royce said quietly; 'they may be anything. They are not regular cow-boys, but they may have been working on a ranche; they may have been prospecting; they may be horse-thieves; they may be regular border ruffians; anyhow, they have got a horse to sell.'

As in all Henty stories there are precise descriptions of a highly informative nature: the cattle round-up, for example, with the branding and method of work. A bronco buster rides a horse three times and then it is handed over for someone else to finish. In answer to the hero's inquiry about such hard work he is told: 'A bronco-buster seldom lasts above two years. They get shaken all to pieces and clean broke up by the end of that time.'

Henty portrays racial feelings often enough in his novels: here he deals with cowboys, blacks and Mexicans. Pete is a negro cook: 'Pete made a grimace as much as to signify that he did not consider the assistance of the Mexican to be of much account. Between the men of these two races there was a general feud, while the cow-boys looked down upon both, and as a rule refused to allow them to work with them except in the capacity of cook.' And here is Henty on the Mexicans:

'That's so,' Bronco Harry agreed; 'a greaser is about the worst sort of white; that is, if you can call them white. I don't know but I hate them more than Injuns.'

Henty's assessment of the effect of carrying six-guns—at variance with a later stereotype of the wild west—is interesting:

'There ain't nowhere in the world where there is so little quarrelling as out here on the plains. You see, if we didn't all carry six-shooters, and were ready to use them, the bad-tempered men, and the hard men, would have it their own way. Big fellows like you would be able to bully little fellows like me. We would get all the bad men from the towns whenever they found the settlements too hot for them. We should have murderers, and gamblers, and horse-thieves coming and mixing themselves up with us. I tell you, Hugh, that without the revolver there would be no living out here. No, sirree, the six-shooter puts us all on a level, and each man has got to respect another.'

Although he makes the life of a cowboy seem romantic, Henty does not disguise the fact that it is a hard life and that not one man in ten is over thirty. He misses nothing: it is not simply the descriptions of the work but the attitudes towards cowboys which have been repeated endlessly in western books and films. Thus: 'I tell you it ain't nice if one does go down to the settlements in the winter, when work is slack, to see people look at you as if you wur a wild beast, who is only waiting his chance to hold up the hull town. Why, I have seen women pull their children indoors as I came along, as if I wur a mountain lion, and was meaning to draw my six-shooter on them just for amusement.'

Henty explains why cowboys lose control after a long spell of work:

'We do carry on,' Bronco Harry agreed, 'thar ain't no denying it. When a man has been out in these plains for six months working worse than a nigger, and that without a drop of liquor, it is natural that he should go in for a high old time when he gits down to a town with money in his pockets; but thar ain't no real harm in it.'

There is no nonsense about Indians' rights; the only good Indians are dead ones: ' "It ain't no good being kind to Injuns," another put in, "There ain't no gratitude in them." ' When the hero, fresh out from England, demurs at shooting down Indians in cold blood, he is told: 'All right, Hugh. You shan't stay with us. When you know the Injuns as well as we do, and know that mercy ain't a thing as ever enters their minds, and that they murders women and children in cold blood, and that if they do take a prisoner it is just to torture him until he dies, you won't feel that way.'

The Henty story-telling requirement that his readers understand all that is happening often produces some strange conversations under the most unlikely circumstances. Thus when the cowboys with some girls and settlers they have rescued are racing across the plains ahead of two parties of pursuing Indians, Hugh, the hero, ever thirsty for precise information, questions Long Tom as to the relative advantages pursued and pursuers enjoy. Long Tom explains that the advantage is always with the pursuers since they come at the pace of their fastest horses while the pursued have to go at the pace of their slowest so that these do not fall behind to be captured. 'I didn't think of that, Tom. Yes, I see, a party that pursues has an immense advantage over one that flies, providing, of course, they are greatly superior in numbers. If not, there will be a time when the best mounted men could no longer ride at full speed, because if they did they would be inferior in numbers to those they chased when they came up to them.' Long Tom gives another reply suited to his sobriquet, and all this as they gallop for their lives across the plains with a large group of Indians a few hundred yards behind them.

When Hugh and his companion, Royce, enter a Mexican area, the latter's prejudices are at once apparent:

'I don't care much for this Mexican stuff with its oil and garlic,' Royce said as they finished their meal.

'Don't you? I call it first rate. After living on fried beef and broiled beef for over a year, it is a comfort to get hold of vegetables. These beans are delicious, and the coffee is a treat.'

It is an interesting aspect of Henty that his heroes are ready to try new things and possess open minds about travel, places, people and customs. Royce attacks the Catholic religion and the easy life of the priests among the Mexicans but Hugh demurs: 'Whatever may be said about it, religion goes for a good deal more in a Catholic country than in a Protestant. It is a pity there is not more religion among the cow-boys.'

The story is a departure from the usual Henty; the author gets the cowboy jargon and manner of speech absolutely right, as he does the other details. Whatever happens in a Henty novel, however, in the end the hero returns to England to a life of high respectability: 'The return of Mr. and Mrs. Tunstall after the termination of their honeymoon to Byrneside was hailed with great rejoicing by the tenantry, who were happy to know that the old state of things had at last returned, and that a resident landlord with an English wife would in future be established in the family mansion.'

Henty's other western, *In the Heart of the Rockies*, is really a travelogue. In his preface Henty says: 'For details of the geography and scenery I have relied upon the narrative of Mr. Baillie-Grohman, who paid several visits to the country in 1878 and the following years in quest of sport, and was the first white man to penetrate the recesses of the higher mountains. At that time the Indians had almost entirely deserted the country. For the details of the dangers and difficulties of the passage through the canyons I am indebted to the official report of Major Powell, published by the United States government.'

Tom is one of the most passive of all Henty heroes and is little more than an excuse for taking the reader on an exciting journey through the Rockies and down the Grand Canyon. Fights with Indians are thrown in. Few Henty heroes show so little development or, indeed, are so quiet and ready to accept the leadership of others. At the beginning, when Tom's mother dies, he is the only boy in a family of girls. He has recently received an invitation to join an uncle somewhere in the United States. The prospect thrills him: 'He had in his blood a large share of the restless spirit of enterprise that has been the main factor in making the Anglo-Saxons the dominant race of the world.'

When he gets out west to find his uncle, Straight Harry, Tom is told about all the attributes he will need to survive and modestly says, 'I haven't any one of them,' a reply that goes down well. There is the more or less statutory Henty admonishment about drink leading to ruin, especially in the West. With a miner, an Indian chief* and the latter's nephew, Tom sets off to find his uncle.

In due course, they meet up with Straight Harry, fight Indians, get snowed up in a mountain range for the winter, hunt, fight Indians again and experience an avalanche. Only one major sugges-tion in all their difficulties comes from the hero, Tom: that they should make a snow fort. Normally the hero makes endless contribu-tions throughout the story; in this case, however, there are too many experienced western men for this to be feasible. Tom indeed displays a more than usual modesty. He is the lead paddle in the canoe going down the Colorado river (they are trying to escape the Indians) when they come to an especially dangerous series of rapids. His uncle asks whether he can manage or whether he prefers the chief to take his place. Tom replies: 'I think I could stand it, uncle, for I have been out in wherries in some precious rough seas at Spithead; but I think it would be best for the chief to take my place this time, and then I shall see how I feel.' It is just as well he does for, at the end of shooting the rapids, he is completely shaken up as, to a lesser degree, are the other men. The chief is treated as an equal through-out and as a genuine brother by Straight Harry whose life he has saved on a number of occasions; they both regularly refer to enemy Indians as 'varmint'. They find and work the incredibly rich vein of gold that Straight Harry has discovered and Tom, his uncle and Jerry become wealthy men. Tom and Straight Harry return to England to make the girls rich and endow them suitably for their marriages.

* The most interesting feature of this story is the position of the Indian chief. His advice is constantly sought by Straight Harry, who keeps saying such things as: 'I reckon you are right, chief.' Harry always addresses the chief as chief. Writing in a race-conscious age, it is possible to see Henty deliberately making plain that the chief is as good as the whites; it opens a new dimension on a writer who, too often, is associated with Victorian racialism—sometimes quite unfairly.

A Henty short story—'White-Faced Dick'—is about goldmining in America. It is unusual. Dick is a timid, ill boy, on his own, who is befriended in Pine-Tree Gulch by Red George who runs a saloon and, indeed, kills a man in a shoot-out after he has hurt the boy. Then the rains come early, the valley is flooded, the men flee for their lives but White-Faced Dick stays when all the others have gone so that he can pull up the mining bucket and bring his friend Red George to safety. He dies saving his friend.

The last American story, *In the Hands of the Cave Dwellers*, is a short novel of only 200 pages. The young hero, aged eighteen, is an American who jumps ship in Mexico, saves a young Mexican who is being attacked by knife-wielding thugs and then accompanies him to his father's huge ranch in the mountains. When the father and son are away the ranch is attacked by Apaches. The daughter escapes them only to fall into the hands of the primitive cave dwellers, the original people of Mexico. Will rescues her and marries her.

When the girl wakes as they cross a mountain stream on Will's horse:

'Where am I?' she murmured.

'You are safe in my arms,' Will said.

At the end—money was clearly a consideration of immense importance to Henty—Will returns to his father in New York: ' . . . where he astounded his father and mother by presenting to them his wife, and mentioning casually that she had a fortune of $200,000, and was joint heiress to estates and property worth at least $2,000,000, which caused Mr. Harland, senior, to acknowledge that Will's mania for the sea had not turned out so badly after all'.

CHAPTER ELEVEN

The Dash for Khartoum

The Dash for Khartoum is vintage Henty and the book has everything: a moral; two equally splendid dashing heroes; a Gilbertian opening with mixed up babies; a section on school life and attitudes to it; a near tragedy; a good historical account of the hopelessly late expedition sent to rescue Gordon; strictures on the incompetence of the government of the day; and some advanced racial views. In addition it is an exceptionally good story.

The title is ironical and aimed perhaps as much at the adult public as at the boys who would read it, for the expedition to rescue Gordon was mounted too late by a reluctant home government and, when it did start out from Cairo, went ponderously up the Nile, almost, as critics were to say, as though it meant to arrive too late. The picture on the front cover of the book of a soldier in full regalia with sword in hand literally dashing (in a hundred-degree Sudan heat) may well have been a joint Henty-Blackie joke.

As Henty says in his preface: 'The story of the Nile Expedition to relieve General Gordon is so recent that no words of introduction are necessary.' The public outcry at Gordon's death ensured the fall of Gladstone's government in 1885, and Henty, whose training as a soldier and war correspondent had given him both an eye for military detail and a readiness to criticize either the generals or the politicians, in this book castigates attitudes at home which made it easy for Gordon to martyr himself.

Continuing his preface, Henty says: 'The moral, such as it is, of the story of the two lads brought up as brothers is—Never act in haste, for repentance is sure to follow.' In this instance, however, without the hasty action there would not have been the superb story that follows. At the conclusion of his preface, Henty again moralizes, making a real point, one that was paramount in all his stories for boys: 'In most cases, cowardice lies at the bottom of concealment, and cowardice is of all vices the most contemptible.'

The story is as follows. In India a Captain Clinton has a baby son at the same time as another son is born to Sergeant Humphreys, who is married to a young and scheming woman who had first hoped to catch an officer of the regiment. Following the birth, Mrs. Clinton is very ill and unable to look after her child, so Mrs. Humphreys fosters it along with her own. She then deliberately mixes up the babies with the intention of later turning the 'mistake' to her advantage, for Captain Clinton is heir to a large fortune.

The Clintons are horrified and, since no one can tell the two babies apart, take both boys on the understanding that both will be brought up equally—the Sergeant's boy thus getting all the advantages of education that money and background can provide—in the hope that as they grow up obvious family likenesses will appear and the correct parents be identified. Mrs. Humphreys is content to have her son taken off her hands—her eyes are on the future—but she quarrels with the Sergeant, they part, he takes to drink and ruins his army career.

We next see the two boys, Edgar and Rupert, aged sixteen, as they pack to go back to school at Cheltenham. Clinton and his wife reflect that after sixteen years they are no nearer knowing which is their son, and the Captain says: 'We have got two sons instead of one; and after all, the idea that there would be a great satisfaction in the real one inheriting all our landed property has very little in it. There is plenty for them both, and each of them will be just as happy on three thousand a year as he would on six.' Although many people know the story, the Clintons have not yet told Edgar and Rupert; they agree the boys should learn it from them soon rather than from anyone else. The boys return to school.

School stories were the rage in late Victorian England and in the twenty pages that Henty now devotes to the school he pokes some fun at the stereotypes. The opening scene consists of the senior boys discussing the house football prospects with a humourless football captain, Skinner, exhorting the others to effort since they have lost their best and heaviest players from the previous year. Skinner takes one boy to task for having no weight; the boy, Wordsworth, says he can run.

'Yes, you can run when you get the ball,' Skinner said in a tone of disgust; 'but if a fellow half your weight runs up against you,

over you go. You must lay yourself out for pudding, Wordsworth.
With that, and eating your food more slowly, you really might
get to be of some use to the house.'

Having dealt with poor Wordsworth, Skinner complains that
Easton is not yet present and, though someone excuses Easton on the
grounds that he has to travel across country, Skinner clearly has it
in for him:

'It takes him so long,' Skinner growled, 'to fold up his things
without a crease, to scent his pocket-handkerchief, and to get his
hair to his satisfaction, that you may be quite sure he cannot
make an early start.'

Skinner proposes that this dandy should be dropped from the team
but the others point out that, once he is in football togs, he plays
well and Edgar Clinton says that he in fact appears to be a good
chap on the quiet although all agree he gives himself airs.

Easton arrives and proceeds to bait a furious Skinner by telling
him how standing in picture galleries in Germany has made his feet
ache (Skinner has been climbing hills in Scotland to get himself into
condition for football). Easton infuriates Skinner still more when he
says that what he really objects to in football is the dirt. Skinner
then suggests they all go for a walk but Easton refuses on the grounds
that a walk with Skinner means rushing across ploughed fields and
getting hot and sticky. He goes off to play rackets.

On the walk, the other boys continue to discuss Easton who turns
out to be a good all-rounder capable of beating most of them at
most things; in the meantime he trounces his opponent at rackets.
At tea Easton chaffs them all for looking hot, one having been
bitten by a dog, another having fallen into a ditch and a third having
been peppered with shot by an irate farmer. Skinner is about to
explode when the house captain, Pinkerton, says that Easton has
got the better of it, something Skinner will not admit. 'Never mind
whether you would or not, Skinner, it clearly is so. Now, let us
change the conversation. For my part I cannot make out why one
fellow cannot enjoy football and that sort of thing, and another like
to lie on his back in the shade, without squabbling over it. If Skinner
had his own way he would never sit quiet a minute, if Easton had
his he would never exert himself to walk across the room. It is a
matter of taste. I like half and half, but I do not want to interfere

with either of your fancies.' This almost heretical view shows a Henty ready to break free of stereotypes although the lines he sets are firm enough. It is Easton's suggestion that they go in for a different type of training—runs every morning to give them stamina —since they do not have the weight; his lead ensures that by the end of the season they win the most important match.

The main object of the school story is to establish the two Clinton boys as first-class chaps—Edgar scores in the game—and show that they have good friends. A strange woman then appears on the scene and watches the boys when they are about the town. It is the Sergeant's wife.

Though she has carefully inspected each one whenever she sees them, Mrs. Humphreys is no more capable of discovering her son than have been the Clintons. In the end she stops one of them— Edgar—and persuades him to go with her to her rooms where she explains what has happened. She elicits from him the fact that Rupert has a mole on his shoulder and says that makes him the Clinton baby while Edgar is her own. She now reveals her villainy. She suggests that she will come forward and tell the Clintons that the one with the mole is her son; the whole estate will then go to Edgar and she will get her reward from him later. Edgar is deeply shocked but promises to think the matter over. He returns to the school, feigns sickness, leaves a note for his brother and runs away. This is where the haste (pointed out by Henty in his preface) comes in; Edgar writes to his brother and parents that, having discovered, as he thinks, that he was fraudulently put in the position of Rupert's brother, he cannot bear to profit by it any more and so is off to make his own way in the world.

Rupert goes home to stricken parents. Captain Clinton institutes a search and puts advertisements in the papers. They do not find him. Rupert returns to Cheltenham where Easton turns out to be a brick. Rupert has told the seniors what happened:

> 'It does not matter a jot to us,' Easton said, breaking the silence of surprise with which they had listened to the story. 'We like you and your brother for yourselves, and it does not matter a rap to us, nor as far as I can see to anyone else, who your fathers and mothers were.'

A splendid view but not one universally held at that time—or, for that matter, later. The seniors agree on their honour to suppress the

6

story and, as Easton says, 'I am sure that whatever he is doing he will always be a gentleman and a good fellow'. Easton has Rupert home for the holidays; things improve when the Clintons hear from Edgar that he is well. Clinton writes to tell Rupert and refers to the fear that Edgar might have committed suicide: 'I have never thought so for an instant. I trust that my two boys are not only too well principled, but too brave to act a coward's part . . .'

Back at school Skinner is reconciled to Easton and apologizes for having been a prig while Easton admits he had deliberately tried to annoy the Philistines. At the end of the Cheltenham section of the book Easton has one last dig at Skinner who by then is reading too hard for his exams: 'Last term it was football, now it is reading. It must be an awful nuisance to be as enegetic as he is.'

Meanwhile, guessing that the army would be watched, Edgar first waits, then avoids the London depots and goes down to Aldershot where he enlists as a trumpeter. The newly recruited Trumpeter 'Smith' resolves not to drink and to win his stripes as soon as he may. The regiment discover that he is a first-class cricketer: he wins a match for them with his bowling. Smith attracts the attention of officers and men alike by his good ways, his cricket and keenness. Then one day when out on a walk he goes to the rescue of two officers' wives who are being molested by tramps and so becomes a hero in the regiment; the officers mark him out for future help or promotion. The regiment sails for Egypt.

A corporal, North, has been picking on Trumpeter Smith; in Cairo he gets drunk and loses his stripes. Smith immediately challenges him to a fight and, though North is a powerful fellow of twenty-two and Edgar only sixteen, the latter wins after an hour and a quarter of fighting—because of stamina. They shake hands at the end and North acknowledges: 'You have licked me fairly, Smith. I did not think you had it in you; but I don't think you would have thrashed me if I had been in as good a condition as you are.' Thus stamina—acquired at school—tells. The fight, of course, improves Smith's standing in the regiment still further. The army now goes into action.

There are some Henty reflections upon the calibre of the enemy: a trooper remarks that it isn't fighting 'against these savages' (they are about to engage the forces of the Mahdi) but he is corrected: 'The Zulus were savages, and they made a pretty tough fight against us . . . These fellows have been every bit as brave as the

Zulus. They cut Hicks Pasha's army into mincemeat, and they have licked two Egyptian armies down in this neighbourhood.' In all his war stories Henty pays tribute to the martial qualities of those the British troops are to fight.

In one engagement Edgar turns back to save the life of his old foe, Corporal North, who turns out a good enough fellow, for he makes a point of reporting Smith's conduct in rescuing him before falling insensible from loss of blood. Edgar is recommended for the V.C. A sergeant tells Edgar that it won't be long before he is in the sergeant's mess and advises him to avoid becoming cocky since his rapid rise must have excited envy in the regiment.

The soldiers begin to learn a healthy respect for the fighting abilities of their enemies. Henty describes in detail the bloody battle of Tamai against the forces of Osman Digna near Suakim. When it is over the British troops embark and sail for Suez. Henty attacks this decision: 'The policy was a short-sighted one. Had a protectorate been established over the country to the foot of the hills, and a force sufficient to maintain it left there, the great bulk of the tribesmen would have willingly given in their allegiance, and no further hostile movement upon the part of Osman Digna would have been possible; but the fact that we hastened away after fighting, and afforded no protection whatever to the friendly natives, effectively deterred others from throwing in their lot with us, and enabled Osman Digna gradually to restore his power and influence among them.' Here again is Henty the war correspondent in action. He now moves on to Gordon, reflecting the popular emotions of the time about that strange man: 'In Cairo public feeling ran very high, and among the troops there the indignation at this base desertion of one of England's noblest soldiers was intense and general. At last the news came that public feeling in England had become so strong that government could no longer resist it, and that orders had been issued to prepare an expedition with all haste.'

The Camel Corps is short of a trumpeter and Edgar through the kind offices of the major (whose wife he rescued from the tramps in Aldershot) gets his chance: he is seconded to the Corps with the hope of early action and the chance to distinguish himself. The Victorian snobberies persist. After Edgar has been given his transfer, 'Several of the officers followed him out and bade him a cheery farewell, for he was a general favourite. All knew that he was a gentleman, and hoped that he would some day win a commission'.

So Edgar is transferred to the Heavies—the Heavy Camel Corps—made up of Guards, Blues, Bays and Dragoons. Henty strictures upon the management of the campaign follow with reflexions as to why some of the heaviest men in the army have been picked for a job especially requiring light wiry men. Like all Henty's heroes, Edgar does tend to know everything; he has studied the country, of course, and is soon busy describing it to the other soldiers—he has got the maps off by heart—as well as the qualities of the enemy.

The Henty style has long gone out of fashion: his wealth of detail is something no modern writer of juvenile fiction would dare include for fear of inducing boredom. Yet it is this very mass of detail—the numbers of regiments involved in a campaign down to the exact number of men and the names of officers or a more whimsical description of camels—which makes his books such mines of information: 'The conduct of many of them was exasperating in the extreme to the riders. When taken down into the stream they would stand and look about in an aimless way as if wondering what on earth they had been brought there for, and would be sometimes ten minutes or a quarter of an hour before the idea seemed to occur to them that they might as well have a drink.'

Now Edgar's personal story moves forward dramatically. He is befriended by a Sergeant Bowen and the two of them are together when three officers pass; they stand and salute and hear one of the officers call another Clinton. The others are Skinner and Easton. Edgar then discovers that Bowen is in fact Humphreys under an assumed name; he reveals that he is his son. Bowen, however, says that the mole was only noticed after the babies had been confused so that it is not certain at all that Edgar is in fact his son. Meanwhile Rupert, Easton and Skinner discuss the campaign and Rupert reveals that he is no nearer knowing the whereabouts of his brother. The threads—apparently—are drawing closer.

Henty makes Skinner go on about football and Easton regret that he cannot have clean white shirts on campaign. Of the enemy Easton says: 'I shall be sorry for the poor beggars with their spears against our breech-loaders, but it has got to be done.' The irrepressible Skinner wants to *play* football; Easton is appalled at the thought: 'It would be fatal to any respect these Egyptians may feel for us if they were to see us rushing about the sand like maniacs in pursuit of a ball.'

Sergeant Bowen, meanwhile, having thought over Edgar's revelations, tells him that he must go on regarding himself as the Clintons' son and that he was wrong to run away and cause them pain. Now, however, he must first go through the campaign since to reveal himself just as he is about to go into danger would only worry them the more. And so the advance up the Nile commences with the two brothers, one an officer and the other as Smith the trumpeter, travelling in the same army unknown to one another.

Henty's humour is not always apparent but in this book it emerges quite often even if somewhat heavily. Skinner remarks upon the value of water after a long march: 'I shall never say anything against water again. I have always allowed its utility for washing purposes, but have considered it a distinct failure as a drink. I recant. While considering that at home beer is good enough for me, I am prepared to maintain that, in the middle of the Bayuda Desert, clear cold water and plenty of it is good enough for anyone.'

Henty is critical of the way the campaign is conducted, thus: 'Nevertheless it would have been far better to have risked another battle in the open than to have made a night march across an unknown country.' It is during this night march that various soldiers get separated from the main body; they include Edgar and Sergeant Bowen who is wounded. They hide near the river but it is clear that Edgar must obtain help so he leaves the sergeant and sets off to rejoin the troops who are approaching in the distance. But some Arabs capture Edgar who learns from them of the death of Gordon. He is taken as a slave to the local sheik.

The army itself, meanwhile, runs into trouble and more battles have to be fought. Then Sergeant Bowen is found, on him two letters addressed to Rupert Clinton and his father in which he reveals that the trumpeter is Edgar and that there is no certainty as to which of the two is his son. Rupert then discovers that Edgar has been taken prisoner.

Edgar's captors have no wish to be soldiers of the Mahdi; they leave the fighting area and head up country. They regard Edgar as a valuable slave. As he runs with his captors through the desert, he muses: 'I thought that a good long run with the hares and hounds at Cheltenham was pretty hard work, but it was nothing to this.' The sheik makes a present of Edgar to his wife and Edgar sensibly makes himself useful explaining the various European items taken as loot. This endears him to his captors and once more he is set to become a favourite. When he is working with two negro slaves, one calls Edgar a Kaffir dog and Edgar reacts as any good English lad would:

> 'Well, look here,' Edgar said in English, letting go the rope, 'the sooner we come to an understanding the better. I am not going to stand any nonsense from you fellows; and if you don't keep a civil tongue in your heads I will give you such a licking as will teach you to do so in future.'

One of the big negroes again calls him a Kaffir and spits at him whereupon Edgar knocks the man down. The sheik sides with Edgar and tells the negroes to leave him alone, and his wife, Amina, says he is her slave and a Hakim whose knowledge of medicines has saved the life of one of her children. Thus Edgar becomes even more firmly established.

Back with the army, the dying Sergeant Bowen confirms on oath to Rupert that his wife could not have known which was her son. The news of Gordon's death then comes through and, when it is clear that the army is to retire down the Nile, Rupert determines to take leave and go in search of his brother. He obtains both leave and help from Major Kitchener, then in charge of the army's intelligence. Before he sets out the army is ordered to retire further to Wady Halfa and so abandon Dongola and the people who had been faithful to the British and Egyptians and opposed the Mahdi. Rupert and Easton are furious and, through Rupert's lips, Henty expresses something of the patriotic disgust which prevailed at the time: 'Our fathers used to be proud to call themselves Englishmen, but, by Jove, there is very little reason for us to be. That Boer business was shameful and humiliating enough [Majuba], but this is worse still. I don't say that we are bound to go on to Khartoum, although it would be the best and cheapest and most satisfactory mode in every way of settling this Mahdi and ensuring order in the Soudan; but I do think that we are bound to hold the river from Korti downwards to protect the tribes that have been friendly to us, and to save this town from ruin and desolation.'

Rupert disguises himself so well that he fools both Major Kitchener and a sheik who works for him and with whom Rupert is to set out on his search. So off he goes.

Meanwhile Edgar finds that one negro slave now respects him enormously while the other, whom he had knocked down, is an enemy. Edgar is learning the language, having determined to escape as soon as possible; Hamish, the negro he thrashed, disappears and the sheik fears he has gone to inform the Mahdi that he has kept a white slave for himself—Edgar ought to have been handed over to the Mahdi's officers. The sheik sets off in pursuit of Hamish.

In a conversation between Edgar and Amina the former reflects that the British may by then have taken Khartoum. The woman responds with some 'inverted' imperial propaganda about the Mahdi, a common Henty device: 'I hope it may be so; before the Mahdi came the country was peaceful and prosperous; there was employment and trade for our camels, and all went about their occupations unmolested. Now everything is changed; trade is at an end, the villages are destroyed . . .' They talk of religion and Edgar gives a simple description of the differences between Christianity and Islam: 'I beg your pardon; we and you worship the same God. We call him God, and you call him Allah; but it is the same. Your Prophet acknowledges Moses and Christ to be prophets. The only difference between us is that you believe that Mohammed was also a prophet, and the greatest of all, while we do not acknowledge that, but in other respects there is no great difference between us.'

The sheik returns with the news that Hamish has escaped and that the Mahdi's men are likely to come; the women and children are packed off to a hidden oasis and the sheik and his men and Edgar remain to fight, building on Edgar's suggestion a zareba (scrub fort) from which to resist. Edgar, of course, is largely instrumental in ensuring not only that the sheik wins the battle but that all forty of the Mahdi's men sent to capture him are killed. So impressed is the sheik that he offers to make Edgar his son provided he accepts the true faith. With great care Edgar refuses: 'Honourable men do not change their religion for profit, sheik. You were born a follower of the Prophet, I was born a Christian. We both believe what we were taught as children; it is in our blood and cannot be changed. Were I to say the words that would make me a Mohammedan, you know well that I should say them with my lips and not with my heart, and I should be a false Mohammedan as well as a false Christian. I could as easily change the colour of my skin as my religion, and you in your heart would be the first to condemn and despise me did I do so.' The sheik accepts this.

Edgar tells the sheik that in due course he will try to escape but will warn him when he is ready to do so. Before he needs to put this promise into action, however, Rupert meets up with them and the two brothers are at last reunited. When Edgar expresses his amazement that Rupert had taken so many risks to find him—Edgar has already admitted his mistake and is ready to return home—Rupert replies, as indeed he should: 'Stuff and nonsense, Edgar! When I found that you had been carried away as a slave, as a matter of course I determined to get you out as soon as possible, just as you would have done . . .'

The boys compare how they have grown since last they saw each other; there is one more fight with pursuing Mahdists; they reach the coast at Suakim where they meet Skinner and the marines. They pay off the sheik, a sum having been agreed as Edgar's price, and he parts warmly with his erstwhile captor. Yussuf, the black slave who had attached himself to Edgar, is bought out by Edgar (Rupert had been authorized to draw any money he needs upon his father's account in Suakim) and asks to come back to England as his servant. They return home to be reunited as a single family. Later Edgar obtains a commission and all ends happily.

The Dash for Khartoum is one of the best Henty novels, for balance, character, moral, history, humour and story.

CHAPTER TWELVE

Rising: Three Morality Plays

A TRILOGY OF Henty stories—*Facing Death, Through the Fray* and *Sturdy and Strong*—deal with the English social scene rather than historical events, although *Through the Fray* is set at the time of the Luddite riots. Henty described *Facing Death* as his own favourite story; *Through the Fray* is undoubtedly one of his best; and *Sturdy and Strong* is a sort of reverse *Eric, or Little by Little*, its hero rising rather than descending. Between them, these stories reveal Henty's (and Victorian England's) obsession with both rising and gentility; they also show Henty at his most sentimental. Henty was a Tory and a paternalist and the fact that he was both emerges plainly from his treatment of the working classes.

Facing Death or The Hero of the Vaughan Pit ('A Tale of the Coal Mines') is a straight morality play: the triumph not only of right over wrong but endeavour over everything. Like many of Henty's stories it is based upon his personal experiences: he had worked for a time in his father's mine in Wales so that the mining details of the story are accurate.

The story is simple. A miner dies in a pit tragedy and his friend's wife adopts the dead man's infant son. The boy grows up with qualities that lead his fellows to call him 'Bulldog'. When, at ten years old, the boy is out walking his adopted father's dogs he meets an artist who sketches him. The artist questions the boy about his ambitions and, when he discovers their extent, says:

'But why don't you make up your mind to be something better still, Jack—a manager?'

'What!' exclaimed the boy incredulously; 'a manager, like Fenton, who lives in the big house on the hill! Why, he's a gentleman.'

'Jack,' the artist said, stopping in his work now, and speaking very earnestly, 'there is not a lad of your age in the land, brought

up as a miner, or a mechanic, or an artisan, who may not, if he
sets it before him, and gives his whole mind to it, end by being
a rich man and a gentleman. If a lad from the first makes up his
mind to three things—to work, to save, and to learn—he can rise
in the world. You won't be able to save out of what you get at
first, but you can learn when your work is done. You can read
and study of an evening. Then when you get better wages, save
something; when, at twenty-one or so, you get man's wages, live
on less than half, and lay by the rest. Don't marry till you're
thirty; keep away from the public houses; work, study steadily
and intelligently; and by the time you are thirty you will have a
thousand pounds laid by, and be fit to take a manager's place.'

This is pure Victorian morality—it worked—which is what the book
is all about.

The boy resolves to get to the top and be a manager; he goes to
the schoolmaster, although he has already started work in the pit,
and tells him he is determined to rise by work and study. The master
gives him more good advice: 'But don't overdo it. You are a very
small boy yet, and it is of as much importance for your future life
that you should grow strong in body as well as in brain. So you must
not give up play. If you were to do nothing but sit in the dark, and
to study at all other times, you would soon become a fool. So you
must give time to play as well as work. Remember, do not be cast
down with difficulties; they will pass by if you face them. There is
an old saying, "God helps those who help themselves!" ' So Jack's
master starts him upon mental arithmetic which he can do in the
darkness of the mine.

Shortly afterwards Jack rescues his friend Harry from an old
mine shaft; he has almost to be forced to accept the gift of a gold
watch for his bravery, exhibiting that essential Henty quality of
modesty. At the ceremony Jack insists upon telling Mr. Brook, the
mine owner, that as much credit should go to the girl, Nelly Hardy,
who was equally ready to go down the shaft to help Harry: the
beginning, one might hope, of a romance. Returning home with his
guardian, Bill Haden, and the latter's wife, Bill says: 'I be roight
down glad, lad, I doan't know as I've been so glad since Juno's dam
won the first prize for pure-bred bull-dogs at the Birmingham show.
It seems joost the same sort o'thing, doan't it, Jane?'

Nelly, who was as reluctant as Jack to be honoured, is therefore understood by him to be a kindred spirit; and so a threefold friendship springs up between Jack, Harry (the boy he had rescued) and Nelly. After the rescue Jack offers to let Nelly beat him since he had embarrassed her by trying to have her brought forward at the ceremony. She refuses this offer and the following conversation takes place:

'What is it then, lass? I know I were cruel to have thee called forward, but I didn't think o't; but I had rather that thou beat me as I orter be beaten, than that thou should go on hating me.'

'I doan't hate thee, Jack, though I said so; I hate myself; but I like thee better nor all, thou art so brave and good.'

'No braver than thou, Nelly,' Jack said earnestly; 'I doan't understand why thou should first say thou hates me and then that thou doan't; but if thou are in earnest, that thou likest me, we'll be friends. I don't mean that we go for walks together, and such like, as some boys and girls do, for I ha' no time for such things, and I shouldn't like it even if I had; but I'll take thy part if anyone says owt to thee, and thou shalt tell me when thou art very bad at hoam.' [The failings of Nelly's parents who both drank were public property]

'Thou shalt be a friend to me, not as a lass would be, but as Harry is, and thou woan't mind if I blow thee up, and tells'ee of things. Thou stook to me by the side 'o the shaft, and I'll stick to thee.'

Thus any possibility of romance is squarely killed by Jack at the start; Nelly is assigned her place as a friend just like a boy and, though she may change, Jack does not: he is to be too busy rising.

Not only does Jack set himself rigorously to learn but by his example he encourages others of the village youngsters to do so, including the faithful, adoring and very tough Nelly. Because of her friendship with Jack, Nelly cleans herself up despite the drunken home from which she comes. One day, a different person, she passes some of the boys including Jack and, though they laugh at her, she is rewarded for her pains when Jack stops for a moment and says to her quietly: 'Well done, lass, thou lookst rarely, who'd ha' thought thou wert so comely!'

The next chapter is called 'Progress' and Jack is shown advancing steadily in his studies and self-improvement. Since he is tough and usually wins his fights he does not become the subject of ridicule

but only of mild ribbing which he takes in good part. Jack turns out
to have fantastic calculating powers.

Then comes the Great Strike. The women oppose the strike
since they and the children suffer the most. One says: 'Talk o'
woman's rights, as one hears about, and woman's having a vote;
we ought to have a vote as to strikes. It's us as bears the worse o't . . .'
Jack is also against the strike.

> 'Well, Jack, have 'ee cum from meeting?'
> 'Ay, Mother; I heard them talk nonsense till I was nigh sick,
> and then I comed away.'
> 'And will they go for the strike, Jack?'
> 'Ay, they'll go, like sheep through a gate.'

Later Jack, who is too young to join the union, tells his mother
that he will never do so: 'I mean to be my own master, and I ain't
going to be told by a pack of fellows at Stafford or Birmingham
whether I am to work or not, and how much I am to do, and how
many tubs I am to fill.'

Jack is careful not to let his peers know that he intends to take a
step up; they merely think he likes reading and can lick any his own
strength in a fight. His master in the village turns out to be a third
wrangler from Cambridge. He invites Jack to tea after his studies one
day when his daughter is there. 'Jack coloured with pleasure. It was
the first time that such an invitation had been given to him, and he
felt it as the first recognition yet made that he was something more
than an ordinary pit-boy . . .' So he meets Miss Alice Merton.
'Jack Simpson will to the end of his life look back upon that hour
as the most uncomfortable he ever spent. Then for the first time he
discovered that his boots were very heavy and thick; then for the
first time did his hands and feet seem to get in his way, and to
require thought as to what was to be done with them; and at the
time he concluded that white lace curtains, and a pretty carpet, and
tea poured out by a chatty and decidedly pretty young lady, were
by no means such comfortable institutions as might have been
expected.'

The strike drags on; Mrs. Haden warns Jack that Bill in his cups
might sell off his books although at any other time he would scorn
such behaviour. When the strike leads to suffering in the village
Jack visits Merton the schoolmaster and bursts into tears at the
suffering of the children; by then he has saved some money and he

gives some to Merton to purchase food for the children, thus also embarking upon the road of philanthropy.

Mr. Brook, the owner, is adamant in his total refusal to treat with the strikers; he says they are wrong and that he will stand out— as he does. It was Henty's usual trick to obtain the sympathy of the reader for the strikers while never condemning the owner or making him appear villainous. Brook is portrayed as an essentially decent, paternalist sort of fellow; the miners as misguided and obstinate but otherwise decent too.

At the climax of the strike Jack gets a warning to the owners of an impending attack upon the engine house; then, singlehandedly, he defends it in the dark, beating off hundreds of attacking miners by the simple expedient of using against them a hose of steaming water which scalds them. It is dark so they cannot see him and he uses his 'educated' Birmingham voice (for by then his teacher is turning him into a gentleman, although at home he only speaks the local dialect). He gets away and the strike is broken.

Nelly, who clearly adores him, reproaches Jack for not using her as a messenger during the dangerous business of breaking the strike: she had guessed that he would try to do so. He is suitably contrite and still—silly fellow—does not see she loves him. For the first time Nelly suggests that he will rise above his own friends and, wiser in the ways of the world (although he protests), says: 'You will try, Jack, you will try [not to rise above them]. Don't think I doubt you, but—' Nelly runs away, leaving Jack and Harry together. Harry says she is going to cry.

> 'Very curious,' Jack said; 'I thought I understood Nell as well as I did you or myself, but I begin to think I doan't understand her as much as I thought. It comes of her being a lass, of course, but it's queer too,' and Jack shook his head over the mysterious nature of lasses.

The schoolmaster leaves the village and a new man with a willing and go-ahead wife replaces him. Jack now takes on the task of persuading the boys of his own age group—the sixteen-year-olds— to go to night school and better themselves. Before he leaves to take up a better job in Birmingham, Mr. Merton persuades Jack to undertake this formidable task: 'Show that not only will they become happier men, but that in a worldly point of view they will benefit, for that the mineowners have difficulty in getting men with sufficient education to act as overmen and viewers. Get them to agree to keep from drink and from the foul language which makes the streets horrible to a decent person.'

Merton sets himself up in Birmingham and invites Jack to spend the weekend with him once a month to go over his lessons and meet his friends. Merton helps Jack buy suitable clothes, and introduces him into his own circle simply as his young friend without any mention of the fact that he is a pit-boy. There Jack talks 'properly' as Merton has taught him, but he conceals this side of his 'advance' from his friends back in the mining village.

The night school catches on and is followed by an equally successful sewing class for the girls. In each case innate prejudices have to be overcome: they have to be taught the advantages of their new acquirements while also working to cut out bad habits of drink and swearing which Henty attacks again and again. This part of the book is, of course, a sermon; but it is delivered like a rousing yarn, which was the secret of Henty's success. The girls, however, regard Jack as stuck up. None the less, the evening classes flourish and the young villagers vie to become members.

Jack buys himself a dress suit. When he arrives at the schoolmaster's in it for the first time, Alice sees him through the window but does not at once recognize him. Then:

> 'Why, Papa!' and she clapped her hands, 'it is Jack himself. I did not know him at first, he looks like a gentleman.'
> 'He is a gentleman,' Mr. Merton said; 'a true gentleman in thought, feeling, and speech, and will soon adapt himself to the society he will meet here.'

So Jack passes his first evening dressed as a gentleman among gentlemen. But his—and Henty's—real secret is revealed: 'Jack would not have been awkward, but he would certainly have been uncomfortable had he not been dressed as were the others, for of all things he hated being different to other people.'

The young peoples' example works wonders in the village so that, when the annual Stokebridge Feast arrives, 'the absence of bad language in the streets was surprising. The habit of restraint upon the tongue acquired in the club-rooms had spread . . .' Mr. Brook, good paternalist owner that he is, gives a rival fête in his grounds quite unlike the usual beer-swilling feast, and the young ones go to it; afterwards, however, there is a riot because the older unreformed villagers attack them for their uppity ways, although, led by Jack, the well-behaved ones win the fight.

Nelly has discovered that she is deeply in love with Jack who does not notice; Harry is in love with Nelly but realizes she only wants Jack. Her parents then both conveniently die and Nelly is given the job of assistant to the schoolmistress so that she, too, is now on the way up. At last Harry asks Jack whether he should not marry Nelly.

'I marry Nelly!' he said in astonishment. 'What! I marry Nelly! are you mad, Harry? You know I have made up my mind not to marry for years, not till I'm thirty and have made my way; and as to Nelly, why I never thought of her, nor of any other lass in that way; her least of all; why, she is like my sister. What ever put such a ridiculous idea in your head? Why, at eighteen boys haven't left school and are looking forward to going to college (though surely not in a mining village in Victorian England); those boy and girl marriages among our class are the cause of half our troubles. Thirty is quite time enough to marry. How Nelly would laugh if she knew what you'd said!'

'I should advise you not to tell her,' Harry said dryly; 'I greatly mistake if she would regard it as a laughing matter at all.'

But even this clue is missed by Jack.

'No, lasses are strange things,' Jack meditated again. 'But, Harry, you are as old as I am, and are earning the same wage; why don't you marry her?'

'I would,' Harry said earnestly, 'to-morrow if she'd have me.'

Harry goes on to explain that people believe it will be a match between Jack and Nelly because they have been walking out together ever since they were small, but the obstinate 'on-the-make' Jack won't believe such nonsense. Harry later asks Nelly to marry him; she says she must wait and hope for Jack, although she and Harry will remain friends.

Then comes the climax of the story, an explosion at the pit, and Jack who by then has acquired superior engineering knowledge finds a way to lead twenty trapped men including himself and the manager out of the mine into a neighbouring pit. There is great rejoicing when the men come out. Brook announces that he will make Jack his new manager. Jack's adopted mother says to him: 'Thou art going to leave us, Jack; and though we shall miss thee sorely, thou mustn't go to think that Bill or me be sorry at the good fortune that be come upon you. Thou hast been a son, and a good son to us, and ha' never given so much as a day's trouble. I know'd as how you'd leave us sooner or later. There was sure to be a time when all the larning thou hast worked so hard to get would bring thee to fortune, but I didn't think 'twould come so soon.'

Jack becomes the new manager; he introduces changes for the benefit of the men and, in spite of his youth, he is accepted because he has grown up with them and always been modest. When he first addresses the men as manager Jack uses his secretly acquired educated voice for the first time in the village and one old miner recognizes it as the voice in the dark belonging to the unknown man (a mystery until then) who stopped the strike by scalding the men. But they do not hold this against him since by ending the strike he has saved them from starvation!

Appropriately the penultimate chapter is entitled 'Risen'. Jack has indeed! It is a Victorian dream achievement: by his own effort, courage and perseverance against the greatest odds. He marries the schoolmaster's daughter, Alice, and at last Harry gets Nelly. The 'model' village of Stokebridge, whose owner, Brook, is a sort of passive Lord Shaftesbury under Jack's direction, now has a splendid clubhouse: 'The men of an evening could smoke their pipes, play at bagatelle, chess, draughts, or cards, and take such beer as they required, any man getting drunk or even noisy to be expelled the club.'

Nelly accepts that Jack will marry Alice who will lean on him; she marries the gentle Harry who needs to lean on her, and these two become headmaster and headmistress of the largest school in Wolverhampton, for though Harry is not strong he is inclined to learning, a habit which, needless to say, he has acquired from Jack. Jack becomes a partner in the mine and a great authority on mining.

Once a year he holds a special dinner at which the artist who had started him on his path is the principal guest. Harry and Nelly are there; his 'parents' who now live in a cottage in his grounds; his wife's father, the teacher, now a professor at Birmingham; and Mr. Brook as long as he lives—he has willed the mine to Jack on his death.

The second of the trilogy—*Through the Fray*—is one of Henty's most satisfying novels. It is set in Yorkshire at the time of the

Luddite riots and, in its examination of the conditions of the poor and the sympathy that is brought to bear upon their case, it has a touch of Dickens. *Through the Fray* is very much a story first with history only providing an authentic backdrop.

In his preface Henty says: 'The invention of improved machinery, vast as has been the increase of trade which it has brought about, at first pressed heavily upon the hand workers, who assigned all their distress to the new inventions.' He manages to show deep understanding for the workers, many of whom became Luddites, while at the same time making his hero a mill-owner and upholding the mill-owning classes, although they provide the story with an excellent villain. The historical accounts of drilling and general disaffection are exact and, as Henty claims in his preface, 'the incidents of the murder of Mr. Horsfall and the attack upon Mr. Cartwright's mill are strictly accurate in all their details.'

A general criticism of Henty's young heroes is their absolute quality: they have all the manly virtues; they have no vices; and, apart from a probationary period at the beginning of the story, usually soon over, in which they learn from some mentor, all too quickly they embark upon their adventures showing a command of situation, a resourcefulness, a mature judgement and a hardihood that enable them successfully to overcome all obstacles. Hardly ever do they show any weakness even though at the start they are no more than boys of fifteen or sixteen. They may grow with the passage of time at least in age; usually, however, they are already set in a mould of heroic capability from which they never deviate.

This is not the case with Ned Sankey, the hero of *Through the Fray*. He is moody and has an obstinate, passionate temper that gets him into a great deal of trouble; he is capable of jealousy and self-righteousness and, by one course of action, does damage rather than achieves the end he seeks. He goes through a most bitter time and very clearly 'grows' in character, experience and passion, so that at the end Henty can say: 'Ned and Amy Sankey had a large family, who used to listen with awe and admiration to the tale of the terrible trial which had once befallen their father, and of the way in which he had been "tried in the fire".'

Henty is generally regarded as a 'flogger' yet in this story he shows himself an educational reformer. The school Ned attends is in the village although it is a 'superior' boarding school. Its master, Mr. Hathorn, teaches by an over-liberal use of the cane; one boy works out that half of them are beaten every day, often savagely. Ned leads a rebellion against him and he is revealed as such a tyrant that he is dismissed to be replaced by a very different character, a Mr. Porson, who is to feature widely in the book thereafter. As a result of the rebellion, however, Ned has first to appear before the magistrates. He is defended by Wakefield, who, after producing a great deal of evidence about the schoolmaster's brutality, says that Ned's attack upon him—he had thrown a heavy inkstand which had injured Hathorn—was self-defence. Wakefield then makes a nice legal point more reminiscent of present attitudes in schools than those prevalent in Victorian England: 'The law admits any man who is assaulted to defend himself, and there is, so far as I am aware, no enactment whatever to be found in the statute book placing boys in a different category to grown-up persons. When your worships have discharged my client, as I have no doubt you will do at once, I shall advise him to apply for a summons for assault against this man Hathorn.'

Ned is discharged and his father cautions him against triumph: 'Beware of your temper, Ned, for unless you overcome it, be assured that sooner or later it may lead to terrible consequences.' Ned, who had in fact been inclined to feel triumphant over his success, is sobered by his father's grave words and manner and resolves that he will try hard to overcome his fault; but evil habits are hard to vanquish and the full force of his father's homily is still to come home to him.

The new master, Porson, astonishes the boys when he first meets them by explaining that he does not believe in punishment as a means of teaching. He says: 'I shall treat you as friends whom it is my duty to instruct. You will treat me, I hope, as a friend whose duty it is to instruct you, and who has a warm interest in your welfare . . .'

The boys listened in astonished silence to this address—and a new era dawns. Henty gives a brief lecture on how lessons should be conducted:

> There was comparatively little of this mechanical work now; it was the sense and not the wording which had to be mastered. Thus geography was studied from an atlas and not by the mere parrot-like learning of the names of towns and rivers. In grammar the boys had to show that they understood a rule by citing examples

other than those given in their books. History was rather a lecture
from the master than a repetition of dry facts and dates by the
boys. Latin and mathematics were made clear in a simple way . . .
In some points upon which Mr. Hathorn had laid the greatest
stress Mr. Porson was indifferent—dates, which had been the
bane of many a boy's life and an unceasing source of punishment,
he regarded but little, insisting only that the general period should
be known, and his questions generally took the form of, 'In the
beginning or at the end of such and such a century, what was the
state of things in England or Rome?' A few dates of special
events, the landmarks of history, were required to be learned
accurately, all others were passed over as unimportant.

The school part of the story is soon over for Ned's father, a
charming figure (a retired army captain with a wooden leg), dies
as the result of an accident in which he rescues a little girl who
has fallen in front of some horses pulling a heavy waggon; his leg
snaps and one of the wheels passes over him.

Ned's mother, a weak, selfish and foolish woman, soon marries
again: a villainous mill-owner known to his workers as 'Foxey'.
Naturally stepfather and stepson hate each other and things go
from bad to worse at home, Mr. Mulready only refraining from
casting Ned out because of his fears about public opinion. Mulready
introduces the new machinery into his mill and shortly afterwards
is found murdered. Unfortunately this is just after a fierce row with
Ned who is accused of his murder. There is much sympathy for
Ned but most people also believe him guilty. He is cleared at the
assizes rather from lack of evidence than because he is seen to be
innocent.

Ned returns home to run the mill on behalf of his younger brother
and sister. His weak mother retires permanently to her room in a
condition of hysterical invalidism, convinced that her son has
murdered her husband. Ned uses the new machinery as the only
way to survive competition yet at the same time gives out extra work
to relieve the distress of the winter. He plays an important part in
combatting the Luddites and helps save Cartwright's mill by his
timely warning. Yet the suspicion of murder hangs over him and he
follows a lonely path avoiding his equals and friends.

There is one exception to this: his friend Bill Swinton. At the
beginning of the story Ned goes fishing with another boy from the

school; they take a short cut across the moor to get home and meet a much bigger village boy who bars their way—he is acting as a look-out for the Luddites who are drilling up on the moors. When Ned and his friend refuse to turn back there is a fight: Ned and the boy grapple and fall, accidentally breaking the latter's leg. Ned then gets help but complications set in and only because Ned's father sees that plenty of good food and wine gets to the boy does he recover; thereafter he and Ned are great friends. Bill Swinton becomes Ned's follower and, for example, warns him about the Luddites. Thus Ned seeks Bill's companionship when he avoids everyone else. Both Bill and the father of the little girl Ned's father had saved are prepared to own up to the murder of Mulready in Ned's place. Bill laboriously learns to read with Ned's help yet, in one almost lyrical passage in Yorkshire vernacular, he describes how he had been to the sea and watched an incredible storm. It has no relevance to the story except to show Bill's depth of character, and his astonishment at a physical world beyond his ken.

When the Luddites break into Ned's mill to destroy it they find him, pistol in hand, ready to fire into an open keg of gunpowder that is stacked upon eleven others and blow them all, himself included, to perdition. They flee. Later his little sister speaks out: 'They are very wicked bad men.' But Ned corrects her:

> 'Not so very wicked and bad, Lucy. You see they are almost starving, and they consider that the new machines have taken the bread out of their mouths, which is true enough. Now you know when people are starving, and have not bread for their wives and children, they are apt to get desperate. If I were to see you starving, and thought that somebody or something was keeping the bread out of your mouth, I daresay I should do something desperate.'
>
> 'But it would be wrong all the same,' Lucy said doubtfully.
>
> 'Yes, my dear, but it would be natural; and when human nature pulls one way, and what is right pulls the other, the human nature generally gets the best of it.'

In the attack upon Cartwright's mill the leading Luddite of the area, Stukeley, is fatally wounded and he makes a deathbed confession that it was he who killed Mulready. So at last Ned's name is cleared. For a year Ned's mother has kept to her room believing in Ned's guilt. Now, in a moving passage, Henty makes her want to slip away because of her terrible remorse at suspecting her son. They meet, however, all is forgiven and she subsequently turns into a most sensible person, while Ned marries Cartwright's daughter. Later, as a highly respected local dignitary, the mill-owning interest in the area persuade Ned to run as their M.P.

The book has much greater depth than most of Henty's: the story is moving, the history is not obtrusive, and there is compassion for the weak and defenceless—both the boys under the tyrant school-master and the Luddite millworkers desperately trying to turn the clock back. The result is a story far above the general level of Henty's more straightforward histories.

The third book in the trilogy—*Sturdy and Strong or How George Andrews Made His Way*—is a Victorian sob-story. As Henty says in his preface: 'Whatever may be said as to distinction of classes in England, it is certain that in no country in the world is the upward path more open to those who brace themselves to climb it than in our own. The proportion of those who remain absolutely stationary is comparatively small. We are all living on a hill-side, and we must either go up or down.' Later: 'And for success in life it is necessary not only to be earnest, steadfast, and true, but to have the faculty of turning every opportunity to the best advantage . . .'

George is fourteen when the story opens; he lives in Croydon with his mother, in reduced circumstances following the death of his father. His mother is losing the sight of her eyes and must go into the workhouse hospital. George is left on his own. For the year before the story opens George has worked as a grocer's boy; now, just before his mother goes to the infirmary, George says: 'I think I would rather do anything than be a grocer's boy.'

So George goes off alone to London and makes his way to Covent Garden where he strikes up a friendship with a street arab who helps him find a place to live. Bill is in awe of George because of his accent, his superior class and the fact that he says his prayers at night in their loft. There is a good deal of talk about God between the two boys, and George instructs his street friend Bill. Bill's theology is of the earthy type: 'That's whear it is; that's what I've heard fellows say beats 'em. If he [God] loves a chap like me how is it he don't do something for him? Why don't he get you a place, for instance?' George takes to reading a chapter of the Bible to Bill (who cannot himself read) each morning before they go out looking for work.

The first break for George comes when he is calling cabs for
people coming out of the theatre. He sees a boy snatch a locket from
the throat of a little girl; he chases the thief, gets the locket back,
returns it to her and then disappears in the crowd. Bill is outraged
that he did not wait for a reward. The girl's father, Mr. Penrose,
says: 'Was he a poor boy, Nellie?' 'Not a very very poor boy, father,'
comes the answer.

Mr. Penrose returns to the market another day with his daughter
who spots George, and then arranges that both boys should go to
work in his timber factory. Bill is sceptical of this new turn but
follows George with devotion. Unintentionally or not, the best
passages in the book come from Bill: 'And I know well enough as it
don't pay to cheek back, not unless you have got a market-cart
between you and a clear road for a bolt.'

George sells his Sunday suit so as to buy clothes for Bill when they
go to work. This makes Bill cry. George then begins to teach Bill to
read. At Christmas, the two boys receive a hamper from Nellie.
Bill says wistfully: 'I should like some beer too, just for once, George,
with such a blow-out as that.' 'No, no, Bill, you and I will stick to
tea.'

Throughout the winter the boys save money and when the spring
comes have enough to rent a small house and furnish it ready for
George's mother, whose eyes are better. She is to leave the workhouse infirmary in April. When George meets his mother and
explains how they have a house for her and how Bill is a part of it,
he says: 'Of course, mother, he doesn't talk good grammar, and he
uses some queer expressions; but he is very much changed in that
way since I first knew him, and he tries very hard, and don't mind
a bit how often I correct him, and he is beginning to read easy words
quite well; and he is one of the best-hearted fellows in the world.'

Mrs. Andrews likes Bill and the house. All seems snug. 'So Mrs.
Andrews read a chapter, and then they knelt and thanked God for
his blessings, and the custom thus begun was continued henceforth
in No. 8 Laburnum Villas.' Mrs. Andrews insists the boys should
change from their work clothes when they come home in the
evenings: 'Company clothes, company manners.' George continues
to teach Bill:

'What seems most wonderful to me, George,' Bill said one day;
'when one looks at them big steamers—'

'Those,' George corrected.

'Thank ye—at those big steamers, is to think that they can be tossed about, and the sea go over them as one reads about, just the same way as the wave they make when they goes down—'

'Go down, Bill.'

'Thank ye—'

The boys earn the gratitude of Mr. Penrose and their workmates for discovering a fire that might have destroyed the whole works; both get scorched trying to put it out while waiting for the fire-engines. The men get up a subscription for them since their bravery has saved their jobs for the winter and Bill persuades them without George's knowledge to buy a piano for Mrs. Andrews. Gentility keeps rearing its head. Thus towards the end: 'No stranger, who had looked into the pretty drawing-room in the evening, would have dreamt that the lady at the piano worked as a milliner for her living, or that the lads were boys in a manufactory.'

The end promises to be sad as anything. Mr. Penrose is taking a party round the works and Nellie gets her dress caught in a machine. In order to save Nellie and stop the machine, George fearlessly puts his foot into the cogwheels. The machine stops at the expense of George's foot which has to be amputated. Mr. Penrose pays for him to have the best possible artificial foot and has him educated. George becomes an engineer while Bill is trained as a mason. Then the two of them go round the world, engineering and masoning together. George and Bill both get married at the end but, interestingly, it is not Nellie whom George weds. In almost all Henty novels the hero marries the girl he saves (and usually has a fortune to go with her).

PART FOUR

Conclusion

CHAPTER THIRTEEN

Assessments

EDWARD MARSTON WHOSE firm, Sampson Low, had published a number of Henty's books, wrote in *After Work* which appeared in 1904: 'Who in the literary world did not know the late George Alfred Henty? Where is the schoolboy throughout His Majesty's Dominions who has not read, or heard of and longed to read the books, over seventy, which he has written for their special delight and edification?' From then until the present time Henty's name has continued to crop up—sometimes the briefest of mentions —in memoirs, biographies or books of reminiscences as an author who had some influence upon the writer. The name means something even if the connexion is dubious.* Some people remember Henty for a particular aspect of his writing which made an impression although more often today he is only a name associated with school, history or empire.† In Canada, Australia, New Zealand and possibly even more the United States there are more people proportionately than in Britain who could say, as an Australian correspondent, 'We were brought up on him for history at school.'

In *Written for Children*, published in 1965, John Rowe Townsend said: 'Geoffrey Trease, in an article in *Junior Bookshelf* in 1952, remarked that the expiry of copyright in Henty that year "will hardly cause the most vulturine of publishers to swoop". Mr. Trease is a shrewd observer, but for once he was resoundingly wrong. Several publishers did swoop, and by 1964 no fewer than forty Henty titles were back in print.'

Some people liked Henty; others found him a bore but an astonishingly large number had read at least some of his stories.

---

* As one ready informant told me: 'I am a great devotee of Henty—*The Children of the New Forest* was my Bible.'

† A typical reaction of an acquaintance of mine when he heard I was writing about Henty was to recall the use he makes of disguises in so many of his books.

In an autobiography published in 1948 Macqueen-Pope says: 'G. A. Henty, whose appearance was that of the ideal headmaster, big, burly, keen-eyed and bearded, was the King [of boys' writers] . . . Boys read him with avidity, even poring over the maps of the battlefields with which the books were adorned . . . A "new Henty" was always demanded as prize, Christmas or birthday present— and always forthcoming.' The use of Henty books as prizes or presents certainly testified to his popularity among adults who regarded him as sound reading for their children.*

Many authors recall how Henty was staple reading for boys. In *The Treasury*, edited by Anthony Deane (volume I, 1902–1903), are given lists from the libraries of four great public schools showing the number of times books by forty-nine authors were taken out over several terms: Henty came an easy first. Hugh Walpole claimed that boys who read Henty were those who sought facts: 'I fancy that all the children of my day who gloried in Henty were the Realists . . .'

The name of Henty crops up again and again in biographies and memoirs even if the reference is no more than 'the school had a good library of books; G. A. Henty, Manville Fenn . . .' In his 'G. A. Henty's Idea of India' (*Victorian Studies VII* September 1964), however, Mark Nadis examines Henty and India at length: 'Henty impressed a whole generation of English-reading schoolboys (and presumably some adults) with his special image of British India. Since imperial policy in late Victorian times was usually made by an inner circle which came exclusively from the public schools, Henty's idea of India fell on fertile soil.'

Most of the people writing memoirs during the 1940s, 1950s or 1960s (in which they recalled Henty) were from the middle and upper middle classes, yet in 1968 in *The Who's Who of Children's Literature* Brian Doyle claimed of Henty: 'His books still sell well today and there are currently over thirty of his titles in print in Britain alone.'

Mentions of Henty appear in unexpected places: in William Gordon's *The Mind and Art of Henry Miller* or in C. S. Forester's *Long Before Forty*. Richard Usborne mentions Henty as reading matter for public schoolboys in his *Wodehouse at Work* while

---

* I have in my possession a copy of *A Search for a Secret*, one of Henty's long adult novels; it has been presented as a prize for scripture by the Primitive Methodist Sunday School whose teacher clearly did not investigate the book, assuming all Henty to be juvenile.

Howard Spring, Harold Herd, Neill Bell, Sir Michael Bruce and Mark Teller all give him a passing mention in memoirs and auto-biographies. Indeed, Henty references recur with monotonous regularity in biographies right into the 1970s. Thus Gervas Huxley in *Both Hands* (1970) says, 'A little later came Henty's historical novels', and Harold Nicolson in *Small Talk* refers to Henty with others: 'These are the great masters to whom I owe my initiation to literature.'

In his biography of Montgomery, Alan Moorehead says: 'Beyond a passing liking for Longfellow's poem 'Hiawatha', *Tom Brown's Schooldays, St. Winifred's* and the books of Henty, Bernard had shown even less than the normal schoolboy interest in reading.' Harold Macmillan in *The Winds of Change* says of his early reading habits: ' . . . but of course we equally enjoyed Henty, Rider Haggard, and Conan Doyle.'

As much as anything it is the range of people who have read Henty which astonishes. Critics may be able to lambast his style or his attitudes but whatever his faults he was read. And mentioned. The late Airey Neave in *They Have Their Exits* said: 'For me, escaping was still a schoolboy adventure reminiscent of the books of G. A. Henty.' Sir Maurice Bowra in *Memories* (1956) says of his uncle Edward from Brazil: 'He was very kind to me and gave me books to read. Henty he thought stuffy, and he introduced me to Jules Verne, Fenimore Cooper, and Rider Haggard.' Early in Kenneth Young's *Sir Alec Douglas-Home* appears the following: 'No less exciting were the story-books available in splendid abun-dance for Edwardian boys and so well wrought that they were still being read by Alec's son forty years later. G. A. Henty was still recounting episodes of history into which he mixed heroism and humour.'

J. Paul Getty appears to have read Henty until he died. His biographer, Ralph Newins, says, 'For adventure (notably G. A. Henty, whose works accompany him everywhere) and for heroes.' There were Henty books in Getty's library and, when he moved, 'they transformed his bungalow into a miniature palace, complete with G. A. Henty'.

A smaller body of writers play Henty down. Neville Cardus in *My Life* says: 'I fought shy of Henty too; I suspected him of geography.' An ideologically inspired attack upon Henty is made by Bob Dixon in *Catching Them Young 2*, in which he claims that

Henty's history is expressed as battles: 'The rights and wrongs, questions of justice and ideology, why so many hundreds and thousands of human beings are slaughtered in Henty's many books never seem to occur to him. The ideology of Empire, far from being emphasised or "justified", is here simply taken for granted.' Later Dixon says: 'Or, *With Cortez in Mexico*. In the latter book, Henty was presumably lured to Spanish empire-building by the greater prospects of slaughter.' Of Henty's attitude towards class Dixon says: 'In *Through the Fray: a Tale of the Luddite Riots* and *A March on London: Being a Story of Wat Tyler's Insurrection*, Henty shows the same bias towards the British working class as he displays towards foreigners. There's nothing surprising about this, of course ... In the long class struggle, Henty conducted a fictional offensive.'

The biographers mention Henty as part of their backgrounds though some, like Graham Greene in *A Sort of Life*, give the reference a point: 'I imagined myself a franc-tireur of the 1870 war of which I had read in a book of Henty.' Other writers use him for literary purposes. He gets his name into an Ogden Nash poem, 'Locust-Lovers, Attention!'. In John Le Carré's novel *The Honourable Schoolboy* (1977) the following passage appears: 'For history, we had *Our Empire Story*, written by I forget whom; for literature we had Percy Westerman, 'Sapper' and Henty.' Harold Nicolson said Peter Fleming 'has a remarkable style, at once fluent and incisive, understands China, and has a jolly G. A. Henty side'. In *The Case of the Constant Suicides* by John Dickson Carr there are Henty books on the shelves of a dead man and the investigator remarks that he did not realize Henty was still read. The most amusing of these literary touches occurs in Compton Mackenzie's *Sinister Street*:

> When Michael was at home, he took a new volume of Henty into the garden and began to read. Suddenly he found he was bored by Henty. This knowledge shocked him for the moment. Then he went indoors and put *For Name and Fame*, or *Through Afghan Passes* back on the shelf. He surveyed the row of Henty's books gleaming with Olivine edges, and presently he procured brown paper and with cook's assistance wrapped up the dozen odd volumes. At the top he placed a slip of paper on which was written 'Presented to the Boys' Library by C. M. S. Fane.'

In a 1974 article in the *Times Literary Supplement*, 'I remember,

I remember', various eminent people were asked to name favourite authors, and A. J. P. Taylor claimed to have read all Henty: '*A Roving Commission* was the best of them, very frightening and full of colour prejudice.' Geoffrey Trease wrote in *Tales Out of School*: 'In 1963 the Bishop of London was confessing in the House of Lords that after fifty years he had still not got G. A. Henty quite out of his system.'

Henty's readability comes across from so many of these comments, whatever may be said of his history or attitudes. There were clearly generations who did not simply read him: they read him avidly and in abundance. In that respect Henty's impact was great indeed.

APPENDIX

The Boys' Stories

7

Publication

In Freedom's Cause
(A Story of Wallace and Bruce)   1885

The Lion of the North
(A Tale of the Times of Gustavus Adolphus and the Wars of Religion)   1886

For Name and Fame
(Or, Through Afghan Passes)   1886

The Dragon and the Raven
(Or, The Days of King Alfred)   1886

Through the Fray
(A Tale of the Luddite Riots)   1886

The Young Carthaginian
(A Story of the Times of Hannibal)   1887

With Wolfe in Canada
(Or, The Winning of a Continent)   1887

A Final Reckoning
(A Tale of Bush Life in Australia)   1887

The Bravest of the Brave
(Or, With Peterborough in Spain)   1887

In the Reign of Terror
(The Adventures of a Westminster Boy)   1888

Bonnie Prince Charlie
(A Tale of Fontenoy and Culloden)   1888

Orange and Green
(A Tale of the Boyne and Limerick)   1888

For the Temple
(A Tale of the Fall of Jerusalem)   1888

Sturdy and Strong
(Or, How George Andrews Made his Way)   1888

The Cat of Bubastes
(A Tale of Ancient Egypt)   1889

The Lion of St Mark
(A Story of Venice in the Fourteenth Century)   1889

Captain Bayley's Heir
(A Tale of the Gold Fields of California)   1889

One of the 28th
(A Tale of Waterloo)   1890

By Pike and Dyke
(A Tale of the Rise of the Dutch Republic)   1890

With Lee in Virginia
(A Story of the American Civil War)   1890

Publication

By Right of Conquest
(Or, With Cortez in Mexico) | 1891

Maori and Settler
(A Story of the New Zealand War) | 1891

A Chapter of Adventures
(Or, Through the Bombardment of Alexandria) | 1891

By England's Aid
(Or, The Freeing of the Netherlands 1585–1604) | 1891

The Dash for Khartoum
(A Tale of the Nile Expedition) | 1892

Held Fast for England
(A Tale of the Siege of Gibraltar) | 1892

Redskin and Cowboy
(A Tale of the Western Plains) | 1892

Condemned as a Nihilist
(A Story of Escape from Siberia) | 1893

In Greek Waters
(A Story of the Greek War of Independence 1821–1827) | 1893

Beric the Briton
(A Story of the Roman Invasion) | 1893

A Jacobite Exile
(Being the Adventures of a Young Englishman in the service of
Charles XII of Sweden) | 1894

Saint Bartholomew's Eve
(A Tale of the Huguenot Wars) | 1894

Through the Sikh War
(A Tale of the Conquest of the Punjaub) | 1894

Wulf the Saxon
(A Story of the Norman Conquest) | 1895

When London Burned
(A Story of Restoration Times and the Great Fire) | 1895

In the Heart of the Rockies
(A Story of Adventure in Colorado) | 1895

A Knight of the White Cross
(A Tale of the Siege of Rhodes) | 1896

The Tiger of Mysore
(A Story of the War with Tippoo Saib) | 1896

Through Russian Snows
(A Story of Napoleon's Retreat from Moscow) | 1896

At Agincourt
(A Tale of the White Hoods of Paris) | 1897

Publication

The Treasure of the Incas
(A Tale of Adventure in Peru)   1903

In the Hands of the Cave Dwellers   1903

With the Allies to Pekin
(A Story of the Relief of the Legations)   1904

Through Three Campaigns
(A Story of Chitral, Tirah and Ashantee)   1904

By Conduct and Courage
(A Story of the Days of Nelson)   1905

In the Hands of the Malays
(and other Stories)   1905

A Soldier's Daughter
(and other Stories)   1906

BIBLIOGRAPHICAL NOTE

The following standard works about Henty I have reproduced, with permission, from the Number I Issue of the Henty Society Bulletin of September 1977:

G. Manville Fenn, *George Alfred Henty, The Story of an Active Life*, Blackie & Son Limited, London, 1907.

R. S. Kennedy & B. J. Farmer, *Bibliography of G. A. Henty and Hentyana*, published by B. J. Farmer, London, n.d.

Eric Quayle, *The Collector's Book of Children's Books*, Studio Vista, London, 1971.

Captain R. L. Dartt, *G. A. Henty, A Bibliography*, Dar-Web, Inc., New Jersey, and John Sherratt & Son Limited, Altrincham, 1971.

Captain R. L. Dartt, *A Companion to G. A. Henty, A Bibliography*, published by the author, Cedar Grove, New Jersey, 1972.

Eric Quayle, *The Collector's Book of Boys' Stories*, Studio Vista, London, 1973.

John Cargill Thompson, *The Boys' Dumas. G. A. Henty: aspects of Victorian Publishing*, Carcanet Press Limited, Cheadle, Cheshire, 1975.

William Allan, 'G. A. Henty', in *The Cornhill Magazine*, No. 1082, Winter 1974–75, pp. 71–100.

W. O. G. Lofts, 'The Biographical Mysteries of George Alfred Henty', *Dime Novel Round-Up*, Vol. 46, No. 2, April 1977 (published six times a year) from 821 Vermont Street, Lawrence, Kansas 66044, USA.

Peter Newbolt, 'G. A. Henty: some notes on the Blackie first editions', *Antiquarian Book Monthly Review*, March 1977, Oxford.

Peter Newbolt, 'G. A. Henty: the earlier books for boys, 1871–1885', *Antiquarian Book Monthly Review*, October 1977, Oxford.

Otherwise I have quoted sources in the text or in footnotes. The many mentions of Henty, often no more than a line, in biographies or memoirs, to which I have referred in the last chapter do not, generally, give information about Henty's life but only record the impact or otherwise of his works upon the writers.

INDEX

(Note: all books cited without an author's name are by Henty)